# Love Stories

# Love Stories

Hollywood's Most
Romantic Movies

D a n i e l  M .  K i m m e l
a n d  N a t  S e g a l o f f

Longmeadow Press

Published by Longmeadow Press, 201 High Ridge Road, Stamford, CT 06904. All rights reserved. No part of this book may be reproduced or utilized in any form or by any means, electronic or mechanical, including photocopying, recording or by any information storage and retrieval system, without permission in writing from the Publisher.

Cover design by Barbara Cohen Aronica
Interior design by Barbara Cohen Aronica and Jan Halper Scaglia.
Library of Congress Cataloging-in-Publication Data

Kimmel, Daniel M.
    Love stories: Hollywood's most romantic movies. / Daniel M. Kimmel and Nat Segaloff.
        p.    cm.
    ISBN 0-681-41400-6
    1. Love in motion pictures.    I. Segaloff, Nat.    II. Title.
PN1995.9.L6K56    1992
791.43′654--dc20                                                                91-36791
                                                                                CIP

ISBN: 0-681-41400-6
Printed in the United States of America
First Edition
0 9 8 7 6 5 4 3 2 1

*D e d i c a t i o n s*

To Donna, for the best love story of all.
—D.K.


To Ruth and Bertram Segaloff, who loved each other.
—N.S.


*A c k n o w l e d g m e n t s*

Grateful acknowledgment is made to the following for their assistance in the preparation of this book: Pamela Altschul; Fred Bierman/Fox Television; John Cronin/*The Boston Herald*; the Emerson College Media Center; Fritz & Sheehan Associates, Inc.; Terry Geeskin/Museum of Modern Art Film Stills Archive; Richard Gollin; Norman Jewison; Joan Pierce, MGM–Pathé; Sidney Kaplan and the members of MAPTI; Jerry Kimmel; Rita Kimmel; Paula Klaw/Movie Star News; Gary Leibowitz; Stan Levin; Helen Rees and Jeffrey Sunshine.


*P h o t o   c r e d i t s*

American-International Pictures
Avco-Embassy Pictures
Castle Rock Entertainment
Columbia Pictures
Continental Releasing
Island Releasing
Metro-Goldwyn-Mayer
MGM–Pathé
Orion Pictures
Paramount Pictures
The Rank Organisation
Republic Pictures
RKO Radio Pictures
Samuel Goldwyn Productions
Touchstone Pictures
Twentieth Century–Fox
United Artists
Universal Pictures
Vanguard Films
Vestron Pictures
Warner Bros.

# Contents

# Alphabetical Listing
# of Film Titles

Adam's Rib
African Queen
Annie Hall
The Apartment
Arthur
The Awful Truth
The Best Years of Our Lives
Bikini Beach
Body Heat
Bonnie and Clyde
Breakfast at Tiffany's
Brief Encounter
Camille
Carnal Knowledge
Casablanca
City Lights
Cleopatra
The Clock
Crossing Delancey
David and Lisa
Dirty Dancing
Doctor Zhivago
Double Indemnity
The Enchanted Cottage
The Gay Divorcee
Gigi
Gone With the Wind
The Goodbye Girl
His Girl Friday
Holiday
Intermezzo
It Happened One Night
King Kong/The Bride of Frankenstein
The Lady Eve
The Lady from Shanghai
Laura
Love Story
Love Affair/An Affair to Remember
Magnificent Obsession

Manhattan
Mahogany
Marty
Moonstruck
The More the Merrier
My Man Godfrey
Ninotchka
North by Northwest
Now, Voyager
An Officer and A Gentleman
The Palm Beach Story
Pete 'n' Tillie
The Philadelphia Story
Picnic
Pillow Talk
A Place in the Sun
Pretty Woman
Pygmalion/My Fair Lady
The Quiet Man
Robin and Marian
Roman Holiday
Romeo and Juliet/West Side Story
She's Gotta Have It
The Shop Around the Corner
Sixteen Candles
South Pacific
Splendor in the Grass
A Star Is Born
The Thin Man
Time After Time
To Have and Have Not
A Touch of Class
Two for the Road
Urban Cowboy
Vertigo
The Way We Were
When Harry Met Sally . . .
Wuthering Heights
The Year of Living Dangerously

# Introduction

Love makes the world go round, and it hasn't done so badly for Hollywood, either. Starting with *The Kiss*—a 60-second smooch that drew gasps in the nickelodeons in 1896—the movies have prospered by telling and retelling how Boy Meets Girl.

Little over the years has dimmed the appeal of that age-old theme, although it has gotten a bit more complicated. Early audiences were content to have the hero and heroine meet, become separated, then reunited for the final fadeout. As times became more permissive, Hollywood disbanded the Production Code office, which used to make sure that even married couples slept in twin beds. Nowadays, as the Cole Porter lyric has it, "Anything Goes."

It's easy to pine for less cynical times when movies featured romance, not sex, and stars wore glamorous clothes which were removed only for a change of outfit. Then the world—and movie audiences—readily accepted screen conventions that would today strike us as contrived. The straying husband of *Intermezzo* (1939) is a romantic figure who still had to be punished for his infidelity. By the time of *A Touch of Class* (1973) he is only a comic character going through a midlife crisis.

If movies reflect the changes that have taken place in society, we should remember that society sometimes takes its cues from the movies. Several generations have turned to Hollywood to learn how to dress, how to act on a date, and even how to kiss. The love stories we remember best are not simply star vehicles (where the leads join in a clinch because it's in their contracts) but those movies that reflect the truth of our own lives.

We feel that the eighty-two films in this book are special. They have survived by having something extra—wit, craft, vision, honesty—that makes them timeless.

As times have changed, love stories have focused on different matters. In *It Happened One Night* (1934) it was unthinkable for an unmarried couple to share a motel room until Clark Gable ingeniously hung the "Walls of Jericho" (a blanket over a rope) between the two beds. By the time we saw *Pretty Woman* (1990), the issue had become whether sex for money could be the start of a beautiful relationship. But even if attitudes are different, the continued success of romantic movies makes it clear that, as Dooley Wilson sang in *Casablanca*, "The world will always welcome lovers."

Making sense out of more than half a century of screen romance can be likened to love itself—a combination of pain and pleasure. Coincidentally, Hollywood's most romantic movies run that same gamut.

In Chapter 1, "What I Did for Love," we begin with those classics in which the characters must overcome great obstacles or make personal sacrifices in order to remain together. Certainly *Gone With the Wind*, and its long-suffering Scarlett O'Hara, is Hollywood's prime example of this form. But so is the more recent *Time After Time*, in which Malcolm McDowell literally travels through time to reach Mary Steenburgen.

A special alchemy occurs when filmmakers leave the studio and set their stories against lush foreign worlds. Chapter 2, "Somewhere, My Love," finds the locations to be almost as compelling as the story: the Paris of *Gigi*, the Eternal City of *Roman Holiday*, the Ireland of *The Quiet Man*, the South Seas of *South Pacific*. In such exotic locales, how can two people *not* fall in love? Yet regardless of how exciting these settings may make romance appear, they can never replace the landscape of common sense through which all lovers must inevitably pass.

This leads us to films that are "pure Hollywood." The lovers in Chapter 3, "Isn't It Romantic," break into song and dance (*The Gay Divorcee*) perform acrobatics (*Holiday*), or literally sweep one another off their feet (*An Officer and a Gentleman*). These movies may not reflect life the way it really is, but they often show life as we *wish* it would be.

Chapter 4, "Hello, Young Lovers," looks at the first stirrings of love. While adults can laugh at their foibles, young people too often cannot. Alas, these very folks who lack a sense of humor

are those who need it most. As this section shows, adolescence is never easy, not even in the movies, whether dealing with the troubled teens of *David and Lisa* or the teen troubles of *Sixteen Candles.*

If, as the song tells us, "Breaking Up Is Hard to Do" (Chapter 5), then many of Hollywood's greatest love stories are about couples who just couldn't work it out. While "Boy Gets Girl" may make for a good movie, sometimes "Boy Loses Girl" can make for a great one. From Humphrey Bogart sending Ingrid Bergman away with "Here's looking at you, kid" in *Casablanca* to Woody Allen comparing a failed love affair to a dead shark in *Annie Hall*, these films remind us that it's better to have loved and lost than never to have loved at all.

But real life isn't all adolescent doubts or grownup tears. Much of the time, dating matures into courtship and courtship frequently leads to marriage. Surprisingly, this is where most movies stop (the exceptions, all too often, are those romances which *start* with a married couple and then show one of the partners seeking love elsewhere). Successful marriages are seldom reflected in movies; happily married couples are as rare on the screen as they seem to be in the Hollywood mindset itself. "Love and Marriage" (Chapter 6) looks at marital portraits such as *Adam's Rib* and *Two for the Road* that depict the joys and pitfalls of matrimony.

Then there are those "Strangers in the Night" (Chapter 7) who let their emotions take them a step too far. Whether it's the world of 1930s horror movies or the litany of deception, obsession and just plain lust in pictures like *Laura* or *Body Heat*, this section presents the dark side of romance, where there are no guarantees that love—or the lovers—will even survive the night.

Finally we offer Chapter 8, "My Funny Valentine," celebrating films that make us laugh along the way to love. Whether it's the screwball Carole Lombard bouncing ideas off the more sober William Powell in *My Man Godfrey* or Meg Ryan pretending she is in the throes of ecstasy in the middle of a New York deli in *When Harry Met Sally . . .*, here are movies which show that laughter is a serious part of a good relationship.

In Hollywood, love is the greatest adventure of them all. But what makes a really compelling love story?

Our primary criterion was that romance had to be the central theme. Plenty of films give the star a love interest, but that doesn't make *Indiana Jones and the Temple of Doom* any more of a romance than *Silkwood*. It also forced us to cut *From Here to Eternity* which, despite its justly celebrated liaison between Burt Lancaster and Deborah Kerr, is more about life at an army base than about any particular couple. Similarly, while Irene Dunne and William Powell are certainly a devoted husband and wife in *Life with Father*, the movie clearly focuses on their *family* life, not their own relationship.

We also chose not to include same-sex romances, albeit for a different reason: Hollywood has yet to produce a gay or lesbian film that does more than treat the subject as a social issue. It may be a while before studio producers simply tell the story of two people of the same gender who are simply in love.

Once there was a working definition, we included films for one of three reasons:

1. Is it a classic of the filmmaking craft whose absence would have been inexcusable? *Gone With the Wind, Casablanca,* and *Annie Hall* are such films.

2. Was the film popular *because* it was a love story? By that gauge we included *The Way We Were, Now, Voyager, Doctor Zhivago,* and of course, *Love Story.*

3. Does the film illustrate an important point about Hollywood's treatment of love? Films in this group ranged from *The Thin Man*'s depiction of a married couple who enjoyed being married to *Bikini Beach* which, while hardly a great film, makes an interesting statement about Hollywood's image of teenage romance in the mid-1960s.

Regrettably, many favorites couldn't be included; if we've left out yours, we apologize. Among the most painful cuts were movies like *Back Street, All This and Heaven, Too, Heaven Can Wait* (both of them), *Separate Tables, Lovers and Other Strangers, Irma La Douce, Love in the*

*Afternoon, Claudine, Darling, True Love, Gilda, Cinderella Liberty,* and *I Know Where I'm Going.*

In the course of our research and writing we discovered that some of the same stars kept popping up while others were conspicuously absent. Cary Grant, with six films in this volume, and Audrey Hepburn, with five, dominate Hollywood romantic movies. Others, such as Marilyn Monroe and Paul Newman—two of the screen's sexiest stars—don't appear at all because their films didn't meet our criteria.

This is a book for lovers. So visit the video store, pop some popcorn, stoke the fire and make (or rediscover) an acquaintance with some of the great romances of the screen.

And best wishes enjoying one of your own.

Daniel M. Kimmel
Nat Segaloff
*Boston, 1991*

# What I Did for Love

*The course of true love is often paved with such obstacles as war, death, fate, and even time itself. These may make it rocky for lovers but vastly entertaining—and even deeply affecting—for the rest of us.*

# Gone With the Wind (1939)

If ever a single motion picture embodied all the passion, drama, skill, and mythmaking ability of Hollywood at the apex of its creative powers, it would have to be *Gone With the Wind.*

More words have probably been written about this legendary film than Margaret Mitchell herself put into its 1,037 pages. People marvel at its intricate production design, the intrigues among its talented artists and the public's enduring fascination that has made it arguably the best all-around *movie* Hollywood has ever made.

Even more ink has been spent analyzing the story it tells of America's Civil War. Essays have commented endlessly on its evocation of a vanished era, its racial stereotyping, and its prefeminist heroine, Scarlett O'Hara (Vivien Leigh), who becomes symbolic of a changing American sensibility.

No one can dispute, however, that *Gone With the Wind* is an extraordinary love story. People cite Scarlett's serial husbands Charles Hamilton (Rand Brooks), Frank Kennedy (Carroll Nye), and Rhett Butler (Clark Gable) and, above all, her undying—and unrequited—love for Ashley Wilkes (Leslie Howard).

But does Scarlett really love anybody? Rhett Butler, the only man who dared think himself her match, doesn't think so. And neither does Margaret Mitchell.

According to Mitchell, Scarlett has only one true love: Tara. It is the plantation and the red earth of Georgia from which she draws her strength, and everything she does over the story's twelve years is in the service of rebuilding it and the way of life that she loved. The irony is that she completely succeeds in saving Tara but does so at the expense of her youth, her reputation and her heart—all of which held such limitless promise when she was young.

It is Scarlett's odyssey in search of love that is at the heart of *Gone With the Wind* and explains why it achieves the level of classic tragedy. Scarlett is a woman who loses everything she has ever wanted and yet emerges as a winner (intellectually, if not emotionally) because she gains self-knowledge.

Remarkably, *Gone With the Wind* is memorable both as a grand and stylish whole and a succession of equally memorable parts. Rhett's first farewell to Scarlett at the road leading to Tara—right before she vows to "never be hungry again" and he resolves to enlist in the war—is an extraordinarily wrenching scene. So is Rhett's squeezing Ashley Wilkes out of Scarlett's mind—and—sweeping her up Tara's grand staircase to make love (in a hideously dated example of marital rape). Or Ashley's woodshed breakdown in which Scarlett finally realizes his weakness. Or Rhett's final departure into the fog, leaving Scarlett alone to plot how to get him back. And so much more.

What nobody likes to admit is that Scarlett is not a very nice person. She flirts, she pouts, she connives, she loves unwisely and she lives to tell about it. But she is also the strongest character in the film (and, in Leigh, far more beautiful than Mitchell intended) and, therefore, worthy of forgiveness because she motivates the best and worst in others.

Her coquettish schemes begin the instant we first see her at the Twelve Oaks barbecue on the April day in 1861 that war breaks out. She is busy deciding which Tarleton twin she will eat with, pines for Ashley, who everybody but she seems to know loves Melanie Hamilton (Olivia de Havilland), and not her, brushes off "a visitor from Charleston" (Rhett), and impetuously agrees to marry Melanie's brother, Charles, to draw attention away from Melanie and Ashley's nuptials. And all in one day.

When she is quickly and conveniently widowed, Scarlett deems grieving to be an inconvenience and longs to dance—in her flowing black mourning gown—at a charity ball. But what man is brazen enough to flaunt propriety and invite her? Rhett Butler, naturally, who revels in Scarlett's unbridled hypocrisy and soon has her waltzing with him among the horrified guests.

From then on, every time Scarlett is in trouble Rhett magically reappears. When she must flee the burning of Atlanta, when she needs tax money to save Tara, when the menfolk raid Shantytown to save her honor, Rhett is there—sometimes to help and sometimes to lecture, but always to marvel at her gall. Rhett is the one and only person who looks at Scarlett and sees a reflection of himself.

"I love you because we're alike," he insists, holding her close. "Bad lots, both of us—selfish and shrewd, but able to look things in the eyes and call them by their right names."

Like Scarlett, Rhett is self-possessed, garrulous, flirtatious and always gets what he wants. More specifically, he is a bastard. No wonder that neither can stand the other for very long.

On balance, there is more sadness than elation in *Gone With the Wind*. There is war (although, contrary to most people's memory, it is never shown), death, cruelty, pain, and incalculable emotional sacrifice. Yet there is also unequaled romance, and with it a kind of contagious optimism.

So when Rhett finally sweeps Scarlett up in his arms and tells her, "Here's a soldier of the South who loves you, Scarlett—wants to feel your arms around him—wants to carry the memory of your kisses into battle with him," it hardly matters that the South is doomed to lose and that their love is fated to fail: we continue to hope otherwise. And as long as we do, *Gone With the Wind* will stay as resilient as Katie Scarlett O'Hara, the red earth of Georgia, and Tara itself.

*DIRECTOR: Victor Fleming WITH: Clark Gable, Vivien Leigh, Olivia de Havilland, Leslie Howard*

# Wuthering Heights (1939)

As every high school student knows, *Wuthering Heights* is one of the most romantic novels in English literature. Bringing it to the movies, however, proved difficult—probably because its highly emotional, quaintly florid speeches, that work on the printed page, seem mushy and overdone when they pour from the screen.

When they filmed Emily Brontë's brooding tale of a poor stableboy's lifelong pursuit of the lady who loves but rejects him, producer Samuel Goldwyn and screenwriters Ben Hecht and Charles MacArthur went for "the good parts." Invariably, these occurred in the first half of the sprawling novel: the private world created by the gypsy foundling Heathcliff (Laurence Olivier) and the ethereal Cathy (Merle Oberon), their romps through the heather-covered Yorkshire moors, and their vows of undying love.

Alfred Newman's lush music and Gregg Toland's low-key photography etch a hostile climate that strengthens people's hatreds while it weakens them physically, so as to make life more fleeting and happiness more precious.

When Cathy—who desires the feral Heathcliff but yearns for the civility of marriage to Edgar Linton (David Niven)—defames Heathcliff, not knowing that he can overhear her, he flees Wuthering Heights. He returns years later having acquired wealth and manners and begins exacting his revenge on Cathy's new family and those members of his own who scorned him.

Sheer intensity drives *Wuthering Heights*. If men and women can hate this strongly, surely they can love with equal power, and such operatic passions form an emotional bond with the reader. On the screen, *Wuthering Heights* creates an additional union by taking place over so long a period of time, and through so many stages of its characters' lives, that by its end one cannot help but be nostalgic for its beginning.

Brontë's novel ends on a heavily tragic note: Heathcliff, having destroyed the lives of those around him, descends into madness and dies alone. Producer Goldwyn understandably wanted something more uplifting for film audiences—a new ending that would recapture the happiness that Heathcliff and Cathy once shared without undoing the moral message of the story. He and his writers eventually devised a fantasy ending in which ghosts of the forever young Cathy and Heathcliff are reunited on their beloved moors. Director William Wyler refused to shoot it, but Goldwyn eventually won the battle. Still, the film fared poorly.

The year *Wuthering Heights* was released—1939—has been called Hollywood's greatest year. Competition, both at the box office and at the Oscars, included *Gone With the Wind, Gunga Din, Stagecoach, Goodbye, Mr. Chips, Love Affair, The Hunchback of Notre Dame,* and *The Wizard of Oz.* Perhaps because of these rivals, *Wuthering Heights* needed several releases to earn back its budget. Nevertheless, Goldwyn continued to take pride in it and considered it among his best productions. He was so possessive that he once angrily interrupted an interviewer who began a question, "When William Wyler made *Wuthering Heights* . . ."

"*I* made *Wuthering Heights*," Goldwyn corrected. "Wyler only directed it."

Goldwyn would probably be pleased that his film has finally become one of the most popular screen love stories of all time. The haunting setting, the attractiveness of Oberon and the young Olivier, and the dignity with which they both read their literary dialogue combine to create a dark fairy tale about a fragile heroine in love with a tall, dark stranger who also happens to be the boy next door. In effect, *Wuthering Heights* has its cake and gets to eat it, too.

*DIRECTOR: William Wyler WITH: Laurence Olivier, Merle Oberon, David Niven, Geraldine Fitzgerald*

# Now, Voyager (1942)

When they talk about three-handkerchief pictures, they're talking about *Now, Voyager*. This deliciously bathetic, consummately crafted soap opera is the quintessential "women's picture," Hollywood jargon for a movie that played best at matinees and—during the early 1940s—on "Ladies Night." Making such films is not easy, as other directors in the genre have discovered; the trick is to take them as seriously as their audiences do, despite the temptation to wink.

Based on Olive Higgins Prouty's novel *Now, Voyager*, the movie follows the travails of Charlotte Vale (Bette Davis), a lonely Bostonian who is institutionalized after her possessive mother (Gladys Cooper) interferes in her shipboard romance. In the sanitorium Dr. Jaquith (Claude Rains) suggests that Charlotte go out on her own. En route she meets Jerry Durrance (Paul Henreid), a man trapped in an unhappy marriage, who lives solely for his young daughter, Tina (Janice Wilson). They fall in love but must part. Back in the States Charlotte asserts her independence, giving her mother a fatal heart attack. Seeking shelter with Dr. Jaquith, she meets Jerry's daughter, Tina, and becomes her surrogate mother. When Jerry discovers the arrangement he vows eternal loyalty to Charlotte and they agree to pretend that Tina is their child. Jerry wants more, but Charlotte tells him, "Oh, Jerry, why ask for the moon when we have the stars?"

So much about *Now, Voyager* is memorable: Henreid's habit of lighting two cigarettes at once and handing one to Davis; Davis's line, "I hate goodbyes!" when she and Henreid must part; her second entrance after an astonishing makeover; and the sheer brilliance with which director Irving Rapper and screenwriter Casey Robinson hornswoggled the iron-gloved Production Code (after all, home wrecking *is* home wrecking). Add to it Max Steiner's portentous minor-key score and Sol Polito's ultraglamorous cinematography and this is an example of the studio system at its most efficient.

The Bette Davis persona has never been more in evidence. She is at once long-suffering, fiercely independent, carnivorously vengeful and intelligently perceptive. Think of what she does: in the course of the film she is a twenty-year-old repressed woman who defies her domineering mother, a sensitive lover, an awakening virgin, a nurturing guardian, and a stalwart ersatz wife. Where did Charlotte learn such skills? Was she gifted all along? And if she was, why did her gifts not surface before Dr. Jaquith stepped in?

In short, *Now, Voyager* was the wish-fulfillment of every viewer who ever dreamed of escaping from a life that had been laid out before her (or him). It was the fantasy of every last-born child anchored to the familial home until the death of a parent. It touched a nerve.

When Jerry—who emerges as the weaker half because he will not break from convention as she has done—offers Charlotte his trademark cigarette, it is understood that she is giving up more than he is. Bette Davis would never do such a thing, but Charlotte Vale would. Nowhere is the magic of the movies more profound.

*DIRECTOR: Irving Rapper WITH: Bette Davis, Paul Henreid, Claude Rains*

# The Enchanted Cottage (1945)

Most actors agree that the most difficult dialogue they ever have to say is the line, "I love you." Despite its simplicity and the frequency with which it is used, the simple phrase embodies so great a meaning that it often ties the actor's tongue. It is far easier to wax eloquent with florid expressions of devotion than to utter those three one-syllable words.

Love can be like that, too: sometimes the deepest feelings are the ones that are seldom or never expressed. This kind of unspoken bond between lovers forms the basis of *The Enchanted Cottage*, a motion picture that may not be as widely known as *Casablanca* or *Gone With the Wind* but is just as dear in the hearts of those who have fallen under its simple spell.

To a cynic, *The Enchanted Cottage* comes somewhere between a padded *The Twilight Zone* episode and that notorious *Dallas* season finale about Sue Ellen's dream. Fortunately for its ever-growing circle of admirers, this gentle 1945 fantasy is neither padded nor notorious, even if it does demand the maximum suspension of disbelief.

Arthur Pinero's postwar play (first filmed in 1924 with Richard Barthelmess and May McAvoy) is a graceful Valentine. In the 1945 version Robert Young plays the disfigured World War II flyer whose love for a homely young woman (Dorothy McGuire) and her love for him make them appear beautiful to each other. The film takes place in a rustic New England cottage traditionally reserved for newlyweds. Only the housekeeper (Mildred Natwick)—a World War I widow who once honeymooned at the cottage—and a blind neighbor (Herbert Marshall) know the truth, and they protect the pair—until the outside world (Spring Byington as Young's meddling mother) cruelly shatters the illusion.

Since *The Enchanted Cottage* is based on benign deception, the success of the whole enterprise comes because we *want* it to happen. Optimism drips from the screen, whether it's Marshall admonishing the lovers, "Enjoy it—it's a miracle—accept your blessing and don't talk about it" or a moonstruck McGuire telling Young, "Listen—it's a song I hear—a melody that whispers all through these enchanted rooms."

Director John Cromwell reinforces this trick visually. Whenever the scarred Young and plain McGuire are alone, or when they ignore others in the room to gaze lovingly at each other, each appears magically perfect. Whenever a third party enters the frame, however, the audience is reminded of the harsh truth. Natwick tells them, "You love each other, and a man and woman in love have a gift of sight that is not granted to others." In saying this, she is including the audience as willing collaborators.

Modern audiences rediscovered *The Enchanted Cottage* as one of the old Hollywood melodramas conjured by the starstruck prisoner Molina in Manuel Puig's novel *The Kiss of the Spider Woman*. There was even vague talk about remaking it for the post-Vietnam generation, but it quickly faded. Dropping it was a wise decision; if *The Enchanted Cottage* were offered to today's more literal-minded audiences, it would probably have to be done with clinically correct makeup and showy special effects (à la *Ghost*). Yet it is the very naïveté of the original that makes this fragile story so enduring. Better to leave it a keepsake, a fond memory. Like an optimistic twist on Dante's vision, the sign above the door of *The Enchanted Cottage* should read, "Embrace all faith, ye who enter here."

*DIRECTOR: John Cromwell WITH: Robert Young, Dorothy McGuire, Herbert Marshall, Mildred Natwick, Spring Byington*

# The African Queen (1951)

Although *The African Queen* is about such unglamorous subjects as a coarse river rat and a middle-aged spinster, it embodies all the ingredients of great sweeping romances and succeeds despite—or very likely because of—its generously self-mocking tone.

Director John Huston and screenwriters James Agee and Peter Viertel (adapting C. S. Forester's novel) crafted the unlikeliest of romances between a grizzled Humphrey Bogart and a regal Katharine Hepburn thrown together amidst the German occupation of North Africa during World War I. It's told in the form of a journey with mythological resonances: Charlie Allnut (Bogart), a derelict who pilots the equally derelict river boat the African Queen, rescues Rosie Sayer (Hepburn), the sister of a dead missionary (Robert Morley), planning to escape the Germans via the Congo River. He discovers that instead of playing the retiring type, Rosie insists that he sober up and attack a marauding German battleship.

As a mismatched pair, Charlie and Rosie couldn't be farther apart. She is proper, he is rough-hewn; she has found the Spirit, he would rather imbibe it. Yet when they share a succession of hardships (rapids, leeches, insects, enemy Germans) they realize to their horror as well as their elation that they have fallen in love.

It is a love that never would have happened in any normal life, but *The African Queen* is no normal story. At first Rosie's interest is more maternal than romantic; she treats Charlie as a servant (Huston suggested Hepburn embody Eleanor Roosevelt) and formally addresses him as "Mr. Allnut."

Only after they survive the river rapids do they rejoice and hug, followed by embarrassment at this display. Not until Charlie frees the African Queen from entangling weeds—and nearly dies of the fever he gets from the leeches that cling to his skinny body—does Rosie's *noblesse oblige* blossom into true affection.

Perhaps Huston's theatrical yet restrained treatment is what makes *The African Queen* such an exhilarating tale of two hearts. According to Viertel, who novelized the filming in his book *White Hunter, Black Heart*, the flamboyant Huston was more interested in shooting an elephant than the picture. Given the director's penchant for heavy-handedness in so many of his later pictures (*Moby Dick, The Bible, Reflections in a Golden Eye*), it could be that his distraction during *The African Queen* is what makes the work appear so effortless.

Whatever. By the time Rosie and Charlie demand to be married by the German captain who is about to execute them, the time for all resistance has passed. A happy ending only wraps it up with a bow. It's thoroughly contrived, but we buy it.

*The African Queen* is mannered at times (as was Forester) and exuberant at others—the inconsistency mirroring the rocky pairing of the vulgarian Bogart (who won an Oscar) and the steely Hepburn (who was nominated). Some twenty-four years later an attempt was made to recapture the chemistry of pairing an odd reprobate with a strong-willed woman, but the failure of *Rooster Cogburn*, in which Hepburn starred against John Wayne, only proved that movie magic, like true love, happens when it happens; it can't be planned in advance.

*DIRECTOR: John Huston WITH: Humphrey Bogart, Katharine Hepburn*

# Magnificent Obsession (1954)

A plot description of *Magnificent Obsession* sounds utterly ridiculous, and yet the film remains one of the classic romances of the 1950s. Bob Merrick (Rock Hudson) is a medical school dropout who has become a devil-may-care playboy, riding around in his speedboat when we first meet him. Suddenly, *crash!* The first of many untimely accidents occurs, and Bob is near death on the beach, in desperate need of a respirator.

There's one up at the Phillips house next door, where an ailing but gifted surgeon lives with his family. They rush it down to the beach and save Bob's life. Alas, it is at this very moment that the surgeon has a heart attack and, without the equipment, he dies. Helen Phillips (Jane Wyman) doubts she can ever forgive Bob.

It so happens that the surgeon was a bit of a saintly eccentric about money, and gave most of his away to needy people, with orders *not* to pay it back. He instead insisted they give it to some other poor soul who needs it. We learn this from an artist (Otto Kruger) who later advises Bob that it is a "magnificent obsession" to resolve to use all your powers to do good in the world. Bob, too, vows to pass on his good fortune to others.

Bob instantly decides to make it up to the newly widowed Helen by giving a large donation to the hospital. Understandably she is insulted, but Bob is nothing if not persistent. He sees her at a restaurant, follows her to her cab, and when she attempts to flee, she is struck by a car and blinded.

Mortified, Bob decides to return to medical school and become a surgeon. He also begins romancing the sightless Helen without revealing his true identity. By the time he tells her who he is, she forgives him and has fallen completely in love with him. But she runs off again, this time to avoid his proposal of marriage, fearing she will become his burden. With Helen's daughter, he searches all over Europe to no avail, but she is finally located back in the States at a small sanitorium, seriously ill.

An operation can save her life *and* restore her sight, but it must be performed immediately. The only surgeon in the facility at that very moment is none other than Bob, whose "magnificent obsession" has given him the opportunity to undo all the wrong he has done.

Based on the Lloyd C. Douglas novel of the same name, the story was so popular that this is actually the *second* version, following a 1935 film starring Irene Dunne and Robert Taylor. (Dunne is something of an unsung Queen of Originals. Several of her pictures proved so popular that they inspired remakes: *Cimarron, Back Street, Roberta, Showboat, The Awful Truth, Love Affair, My Favorite Wife, A Guy Named Joe,* and *Anna and The King of Siam.*)

Produced by Ross Hunter and directed by Douglas Sirk, *Magnificent Obsession* is done with absolute conviction. At no time do they condescend to the material or wink at the audience. They *believe* in Bob's quest just as the audience wants to believe, and if his epiphany is accompanied by the chorale from Beethoven's Ninth Symphony, so much the better.

Rock Hudson had been around since 1948 making forgettable movies like *I Was a Shoplifter* and *Taza, Son of Cochise.* It took *Magnificent Obsession* to turn him into a star. Wyman, who won an Oscar for her performance in *Johnny Belinda* (1948), was nominated yet again, losing to Grace Kelly in *The Country Girl.* The success of the film led the producer, director, and stars to be reunited the following year for *All That Heaven Allows.*

Hokey as it sounds, *Magnificent Obsession* works because it never loses sight of its belief in the redemptive power of love. Such movies are often dismissed as "three-hanky pictures," but no less a serious filmmaker than the late German director Rainer Werner Fassbinder (*The Marriage of Maria Braun*) cited director Douglas Sirk as one of his major influences.

*DIRECTOR: Douglas Sirk WITH: Jane Wyman, Rock Hudson, Agnes Moorehead, Otto Kruger*

# Picnic (1955)

In *Picnic* most of the characters see love as the magic tonic that will solve their problems. William Inge's play *Picnic*, adapted to the screen by director Joshua Logan and screenwriter Daniel Taradash, promises no cures, but it does remind us that those who never take any risks will never gain their heart's desires.

When Hal (William Holden) drifts into town on Labor Day he is recognized by old friend Allan Benson (Cliff Robertson in his screen debut), a rich boy who feels he'll never measure up to his father's expectations. Hal is welcomed as a guest rather than a stranger by the people preparing for the town's big annual picnic. He toys with the idea of finally settling down, telling them, "There comes a time in a man's life when he's got to stop rolling around like a pinball."

Madge (Kim Novak) is the town beauty, who is expected to marry Allan. It isn't the sort of life she would choose for herself, but she doesn't see any other options. Hal's arrival suddenly presents her with a choice.

The film's big moment is their dance together after she has been crowned Queen of Neewollah (Halloween spelled backwards). Hal has been entertaining her adolescent sister Millie (Susan Strasberg) and is trying to teach her a new dance step. "I wish I could do it," Millie says.

Madge steps in, and everyone is breathless as they dance together. As with the Astaire-Rogers films, this dance is a metaphor—in this case for the sort of adult relationship for which Millie is not yet ready. Hal and Madge make beautiful music together. Later, Madge tells him how awkward and uncomfortable she usually feels when she dances with the boys in town, "But with you I had the feeling you knew exactly what you were doing, and I could follow you every step of the way."

Hal and Madge enable each other to break out of their shells so that when Hal is forced to flee at the end (a jealous Allan is trying to have him arrested), Madge has the courage to pick herself up and leave town. They will presumably try to make it work out between them, but even if they fail, their love has given them the power to overcome the fear that there was nothing they could do to change their lives.

Their story is balanced by Howard (Arthur O'Connell) and Rosemary (Rosalind Russell), a middle-aged couple who can't make the commitment to get married. The scene in which Rosemary pleads with Howard to marry her is tragic because she's desperately trying to change her life while he's already given up the fight. "A person forms certain ways of living," says Howard, "and one day it's too late to change."

Earlier, drunk and angry, Rosemary had danced with Hal and ended up ripping his shirt. She tells Hal off in a bitter speech about how he'll end up in the gutter all alone, but the truth is she's really angry at herself. She pleads for love to fill up the empty spaces in her life but doesn't seem to know how to give it in return.

Perhaps that's where Hal and Madge will succeed. Both feel inadequate, with Hal claiming "there's no place in the world for a guy like me" and Madge "so tired of just being told I'm pretty." Yet they each reach out to help the *other*. If there is redemption to be found in romance, *Picnic* tells us, it is in moments where one's partner becomes more important than oneself.

*DIRECTOR: Joshua Logan WITH: William Holden, Kim Novak, Rosalind Russell, Arthur O'Connell, Cliff Robertson, Susan Strasberg*

# Marty (1955)

*M*arty is the film Hollywood pointed to for the twenty-one years before *Rocky* to show that a little picture with no stars could come out of nowhere and be a hit—inevitably forgetting that, in Hollywood, little pictures with no stars only get made by accident.

In the case of *Marty* it was because Paddy Chayefsky's critically hailed TV drama was brought to the big screen by powerful producers Harold Hecht and Burt Lancaster and visionary distributor United Artists—the first time a television show was remade as a movie.

It was nothing more than the story of Marty, a Bronx butcher who unexpectedly finds love with a plain girl, Clara, after having long ago given up hope. Despite his mother's fear of loneliness and his friends' chiding that she is "a dog," Marty says, "All I know is, I had a good time last night!" and phones Clara for a second date.

Legend has it that Chayefsky had originally created the role for—and may have based it partly on—Martin Ritt, a burly New York actor whom the network refused to hire because his name appeared on the McCarthy-era blacklist (Ritt later became the director of *Hud*, *Sounder*, and *Norma Rae*). When Ritt proved unacceptable to the network, another young actor, Rod Steiger, was hurriedly cast.

For the film, Ernest Borgnine replaced Steiger, who had become a sensation with *On the Waterfront* the year before. Betsy Blair replaced Nancy Marchand as Clara, and Esther Minciotti recreated her role as Marty's long-suffering mother. Delbert Mann, who had directed the television production, was given the chance to make its screen counterpart. The critics loved it, audiences followed suit, and the Academy of Motion Picture Arts and Sciences marveled at the charm and power of this modest black-and-white drama that had survived the onslaught of other studios' Technicolor and CinemaScope spectaculars. Mann, Chayefsky, Borgnine, and the film itself all won Oscars.

Despite its optimistic theme, *Marty* is really about the *absence* of love. Marty's friends seek "a good time," not commitment, from the women they pick up. His cousin Tommy (Jerry Paris) is in a troubled marriage made worse by his widowed mother, Marty's Aunt Katarina, living in his home. Marty's mother, also a widow, misses her husband and cooking for her other four children, who are all married and gone.

As for Clara, who lives in Brooklyn, she has been ditched so often that when Marty meets her at the Stardust Ballroom she is astonished that anyone could still be interested. They discover that they share a loneliness and don't realize that each is the other's way out.

"Dogs like us, we ain't such dogs as we think we are," he tells her, almost having an epiphany.

*Marty* strives for simplicity and is never disingenuous in achieving it. Chayefsky creates his earthy characters cleanly and compassionately, and director Mann is content to let the camera simply rest on them talking—not pounding it home but just watching them behave the way real people do, or try to do. The timelessness of *Marty* comes from the universality of its theme and from the complete lack of pretense it shows in addressing this theme.

But beyond all that, it is a hopeful story about average people with average goals and average means of achieving them. *Marty* is one movie where it's not like in the movies, it's like in real life.

*DIRECTOR: Delbert Mann WITH: Ernest Borgnine, Betsy Blair*

# The Apartment (1960)

In terms of a romantic *comedy, The Apartment* would not initially seem to hold a great deal of promise. C.C. Baxter (Jack Lemmon) is a very junior employee in a massive company who is playing up to his bosses by lending them his apartment for their extramarital trysts. Fran Kubelik (Shirley MacLaine) is an elevator operator in the building who is the latest in the long line of "other women" for the unscrupulous Jeff Sheldrake (Fred MacMurray). C.C. has a crush on Fran, and they start to build a relationship after she tries to commit suicide in his apartment on Christmas Eve.

This is the stuff of tragedy, not comedy, unless it is in the capable hands of writer-director Billy Wilder and cowriter I. A. L. Diamond. The film walked away with several Oscars, including Best Picture, Best Director, and Best Screenplay. Wilder and Diamond depict C.C. not as a proto-yuppie, similar to the philandering executives whom he is trying to join, but as "some shnook" of whom his bosses can take advantage.

They promise him that he's on his way up the corporate ladder, but all he gets to deal with are empty liquor bottles, full ashtrays and complaints from the neighbors, who think *he's* responsible for the wild goings-on. C.C. does get his big break when Mr. Sheldrake proclaims him "executive material," but it's only so long as no one other than Sheldrake gets the spare key to C.C.'s apartment.

Sheldrake is also exploiting Fran. "You see a girl a couple of times a week and right away they think you're going to divorce your wife," he confides to C.C., his new second administrative assistant. When C.C. discovers the comatose Fran in his apartment, he is the loyal underling, immediately notifying Sheldrake at home. "I thought maybe you'd like to be here when she woke up."

Instead, Sheldrake brushes him off with "No, you'll have to handle it. In fact, I'm counting on you."

It is at this point that C.C. and Fran discover the possibility for an honest romance, rather than another of the furtive relationships they have encouraged. We see that, in many ways, these two characters are cut from the same cloth. Both are upwardly mobile (he in the company, she literally—as an elevator operator). Both have been used by Sheldrake. Both have trouble counting: when he's asked at the company Christmas party how many drinks he's had, he answers, "Three," while holding up four fingers. She does the same thing later when he asks her how many men there have been in her life.

They both share a love for gin rummy, which becomes the language in which they can finally communicate. It is through gin rummy that he helps her recuperate from the suicide attempt. It is also through the card game that he accidentally gets the punishment his amoral behavior has long deserved. Fran's muscular brother-in-law (Johnny Seven) eventually socks him after hearing C.C. say to Fran, "I don't want to take advantage of you the way I did yesterday in bed," not realizing that C.C. is talking about one of their card games.

Surviving this ordeal, both Fran and C.C. gain the courage to write off the oily and shallow Sheldrake. After the two realize they have found each other at last, C.C. attempts to proclaim his true feelings, using the same words Fran has undoubtedly heard so many times as to render them meaningless.

"Shut up and deal," she says with a smile as they sit down to resume their gin rummy game.

*DIRECTOR: Billy Wilder WITH: Jack Lemmon, Shirley MacLaine, Fred MacMurray, Edie Adams*

# Cleopatra (1963)

The most torrid love affair going on in *Cleopatra* was not the one up on the screen but the one behind it. As a result, thanks to all the headlines its stars generated at the time, most people are inclined to forget that it is a remarkably good picture that only accidentally destroyed one studio, two marriages and several careers.

*Cleopatra* is neither as bad as people say it is nor as good as it was supposed to be. An uneasy amalgam of histories by Plutarch, Appianus, Suetonius and Charles Marie Franzero; screenwriters Sidney Buchman, Lawrence Durrell and Ranald MacDougall; and harried writer-director Joseph L. Mankiewicz, the film is, unfortunately, better known as the one that Liz and Dick were making when she left Eddie for him and he ditched his wife Sybil, for her.

The battle of *Cleopatra* has been so well chronicled that it's easy to forget its importance as a monumental love story and an exceptionally literate screen epic.

The story takes twenty years to unfold and over four hours to watch (cut after release, it has now been restored on video). It begins as nineteen-year-old Queen Cleopatra of Egypt (Elizabeth Taylor) is visited by Emperor Julius Caesar of Rome (Rex Harrison) to resolve her civil war with her brother, Ptolemy. She captivates Caesar and together they dream of a new world order that they will share. When Caesar is assassinated, General Mark Antony takes his place first in Egypt and then in Cleopatra's bed. Antony's bitter dispute with Caesar's son, Octavian (Roddy McDowall), sparks war, and now fighting more for Cleopatra than for Rome, Antony is disgraced in battle and commits suicide. On learning her lover's fate, Cleopatra too takes her own life.

Given its size and weight, it's astonishing that *Cleopatra*, has any light moments but it does, particularly in its first half. Most of them belong to Taylor: her presentation to Caesar, unrolled from a carpet at his feet—is a winning introduction. So is her attention-grabbing entrance into the Roman Forum, which is played as gargantuan spectacle with Taylor atop a huge Sphinx dragged by three hundred Nubian slaves as thousands of extras cheer amidst colored smoke and soaring streamers. Then, she descends from her perch and greets Caesar with a playful wink.

In the restored *Cleopatra* one clearly sees that the Queen is not a conniving minx but a skilled political strategist who beguiles Rome's two most powerful men with an irresistible blend of sex and power. The fact that great armies fight because of it is the sort of footnote that history always whispers but never proves. It also says that men make war when they can't make love, and that nothing wins a woman's affection like a military victory.

If this sounds like epic misogyny, it may also explain why the Queen of the Nile holds such fascination, and why *Cleopatra* is such a startling film.

"I will not have love as my master," Cleopatra tells Antony, rejecting his earliest entreaties, to which he responds, "Then you will not have me." By the end of their tryst she is telling him, "Without you, Antony, this is not a world I want to live in, much less conquer." With lines like that—played out by stars who the world knew were rehearsing them in private—small wonder that for nearly three decades people have been watching *Cleopatra* for reasons other than what's on the screen.

In the end, Mankiewicz called *Cleopatra* "the hardest three pictures I ever made" and to this day reportedly refuses to speak its title. He's cheating himself out of credit for understanding history in a way better than the historians. In his intricate, sexually charged film he portrays legendary figures as people first and world leaders second. In so doing, he brings them to life.

The fact that this $40 million blockbuster (and it did bust Twentieth Century–Fox's block) is barely dated is tribute to its gall. Mankiewicz, Taylor, Burton and Harrison remembered that battles may be fought during the day, but history is made at night.

*DIRECTOR-COWRITER: Joseph L. Mankiewicz WITH: Elizabeth Taylor, Richard Burton, Rex Harrison*

# Robin and Marian (1976)

The generation that grew up on the romance and happy endings of movies like *The Adventures of Robin Hood* (1938), with Errol Flynn and Olivia de Havilland, sometimes wondered what happened *after* "they lived happily ever after." In *Robin and Marian* director Richard Lester and writer James Goldman answered that question by looking at the later days of Robin Hood and the Maid Marian, and the result is bittersweet.

Robin (Sean Connery) has grown weary, having spent the past twenty years on the Crusades and related battles with King Richard the Lionhearted (Richard Harris). When the King dies, Robin and Little John (Nicol Williamson) return to Sherwood Forest, only to find that England has changed greatly in their absence. Perhaps the most startling change is that Marian (Audrey Hepburn, in her first role since 1967's *Wait Until Dark*) has taken vows and is now the abbess at a nearby convent.

"Lovely girl, haven't thought of her in years," muses Robin, and she echoes his remark. On the contrary, hardly a day has gone by that they haven't remembered each other. When she later asks him if there were many women in his life, he answers, "Yes, but they all looked like you."

The early portion of the film is a comic adventure, and their romance follows along those lines as they rediscover each other and rekindle their old affection. "You never wrote," she complains at one point, but she has no answer when he confesses, simply, "I don't know how."

The story soon turns dark. King John (Ian Holm) is feuding with the Pope, and Marian has become a pawn in the game. The Sheriff of Nottingham (Robert Shaw) is supposed to arrest her, and she is willing to submit, but Robin can't conceive of *not* rescuing her from his old nemesis. Oddly, it is Robin and the Sheriff who most clearly understand each other in a world that has already bypassed both of them.

Robin defeats the Sheriff in the end. *Robin and Marian* isn't *that* revisionist, but our romantic figures are now old in a world where life was often cut short by disease and war. Robin still sees himself as a young hero, but he must admit that he is also an old man with a lifetime of regrets. "I'd be twenty for you if I could," says Marian, but not even legends get to turn back the clock.

Dying from his wounds, Robin is given a poison by Marian to numb the pain. Marian takes some as well. If they can't be together in life, they will be together in death. Their final moments are painful, as they try—and fail—to reach out to each other. Little John hands Robin his bow and arrow, and Robin instructs him to bury them where the arrow lands. We never see the arrow fall to earth. Instead it flies off into eternity.

Perhaps the movie divided audiences because instead of tying everything up with a happy ending, it reminds us of the difference between facing reality and imagining the world as we would like it to be. Faced with the conflict between legend and reality, *Robin and Marian* finally opts for the perfection of legend. Ironically, in order to achieve immortality, the lovers first have to die.

But there isn't a viewer of any of the Robin Hood films, including 1991's *Robin Hood: Prince of Thieves*, with Kevin Costner and Mary Elizabeth Mastrantonio, who isn't convinced that Robin and Marian will *always* be together.

*DIRECTOR: Richard Lester WITH: Sean Connery, Audrey Hepburn, Nicol Williamson, Robert Shaw, Richard Harris, Ian Holm*

# Time After Time (1979)

One doesn't usually turn to science fiction films for romance. Usually the women in such movies are mere adjuncts to the hero, with actresses from Faith Domergue in *This Island Earth* (1954) to Geena Davis in *The Fly* (1986) doing their best with a part in which the greatest challenge is yelling in fright at the monster/alien/robot.

Writer-director Nicholas Meyer puts romance at the center of *Time After Time* by anachronistically sending both H. G. Wells (Malcolm McDowell) and Jack The Ripper (David Warner) ahead from 1880s London to 1979 San Francisco. He had already written the Sherlock-Holmes-meets-Sigmund-Freud plot of *The Seven Per Cent Solution*, and would later send the cast of *Star Trek IV* (1986) *back* to twentieth-century San Francisco.

Wells pursues the Ripper via Wells' time machine, a creation attributed to him through his authorship of the novel *The Time Machine*. Realizing that no one in 1979 will believe his incredible story, Wells enlists the help of Amy Robbins (Mary Steenburgen), a bank officer who handles foreign exchange and knows where the Ripper is.

For Amy, a liberated woman of her era, it is love at first sight, and she's not about to let him get away. (Apparently it was love at first sight off camera, too. Although they later separated, McDowell and Steenburgen married after meeting on the film.)

Meyer has three things on his mind here. One is the adventure of Wells pursuing the Ripper, who is revealed to be a surgeon and an intimate of Wells's back in nineteenth-century London. "You're a regular Sherlock Holmes," says Jack admiringly, when Wells discovers his hideout.

Another is the strange view that a Victorian would have of late-twentieth-century America, from Hare Krishnas to telephones to our failure to solve the problem of violence. Expecting perfection in the future, Wells's first reaction to Jack's flight is, "What have I done? Let that bloody maniac loose on utopia!"

Most important, though, is the relationship between the forward-looking Wells and the modern-thinking Amy. She's touched by what she calls his "little-boy-lost routine," which she says brings out her maternal instincts. He is forced to admit that he is, indeed, lost. Yet in spite of the gap of nearly a century between them, they are very much alike.

"He wanted me to give up work and have children," says Amy of her ex-husband. "The housewife routine."

"I'm divorced for a similar reason," replies Wells. "She wanted me to *be* routine."

Yet Amy has to be the aggressor in their relationship, because Wells—in spite of his advocacy of "free love" in his writings—is positively Victorian in his actions. In the middle of a seduction he stops to make sure she is not being "compromised." She tells him, "If you don't take me in your arms this very minute, I'll scream."

In the end good triumphs over evil and the couple realize that they have to face a unique "my place or yours" problem: deciding where to go in time.

"Every age is the same," says Wells. "It's only love that makes any of them bearable." Still he feels he must return to complete his work. Having already won his admission that *her* career is of equal importance, she decides at literally the last moment to give up the present and return with him to 1893 London.

As they take off together, it's hard to say which is the more romantic notion: characters traveling back and forth in time or two people overcoming all the odds to find, and keep, their perfect mate.

*DIRECTOR: Nicholas Meyer WITH: Malcolm McDowell, Mary Steenburgen, David Warner*

# She's Gotta Have It (1986)

I t's easy to forget that Spike Lee, who wrote and directed such kinetic and confrontational films as *Do the Right Thing*, *Jungle Fever*, and *School Daze*, first hit the public consciousness with the restrained, downright touching *She's Gotta Have It* in 1986. This fragmented (à la *Annie Hall*), narrative-jumping charmer followed layout and paste-up artist Nola Darling (Tracy Camilla Johns) and her three lovers: protective and possessive Jamie (Redmon Hicks); self-centered mentor Greer (John Canada Terrell); and childish but devoted Mars (Spike Lee).

As with her career, Nola's love life is also a collage. She is drawn to all three men (and there have been, by her admission, many others, earning her the reputation as a "freak," a term she despises), yet not exclusively to any one of them.

In turn, all three men are drawn to her, and Lee's stroke of genius in *She's Gotta Have It* has them explain why to the camera, not to Nola—the irony being that if they would only pour out their hearts to the woman they love instead of the audience there would be some basis for a true relationship.

But Nola isn't sure what she wants, either, so she wants it all. The suave Greer would teach her style (not that she doesn't already have it) and good loving, but little else. Life with Mars would never be dull, but it would always be infantile. Only the sensitive but wimpy Jamie has promise, but she stalls him just a little too long.

*She's Gotta Have It* addresses issues that divide the African-American community: self-image, sexual attitudes, and male and female identity. Coming after two decades of exploitation movies, it does so with unusual lucidity, and it's not always pretty.

"The decent black men are all taken," a group of black women pines in a nightmare Nola has while choosing among her beaux. "The rest are in prison or homos." Despite this battle cry, she still refuses to decide, eventually realizing that there's no reason (except societal pressure) why she should. Her only problem is convincing Jamie, who by now has given up on her, to try again—a decision that leads to virtual rape in the film's most controversial and disturbing moment.

The issues of how black men view black women and how black women view themselves form the fabric of the film. Nola's male friends provide sex, while her female friends offer succor: former roommate Clorinda Bradford (Joie Lee) knows Nola's habits, and lesbian friend Opal Gilstrep (Raye Dowell) knows her heart, although Nola makes a point of rejecting her.

Otherwise, it's often hard to tell what's on Lee's agile directorial mind; his hard-edged ideas clash mightily with his performers' uniformly weak acting. While Ernest Dickerson's stalking camera imparts visual vitality, much of the film's verve was achieved in the editing, not the shooting (Lee has since more than brought his directing up to the level of his other skills). The only performance that is effective is, not surprisingly, Lee's own bicycle messenger, Mars. His mantra-like "Please baby, please baby, please baby, baby please" is the best pickup line since "What's your sign?"

There is still gloss, and it makes its point. In the black and white film's lone color sequence, Jamie stages a birthday concert for Nola in a park only blocks away from their Bedford-Stuyvesant neighborhood. It's a Hollywood-style dance duet set not on a soundstage but in the real world. The bright colors contrast with the modern background as if to ask whether old ideas can survive in this brave new world that films like *She's Gotta Have It* have ushered in.

*DIRECTOR-WRITER-EDITOR: Spike Lee WITH: Tracy Camilla Johns, Redmon Hicks, John Canada Terrell, Spike Lee*

# CHAPTER TWO

# Somewhere, My Love

*In Hollywood's eyes love is more meaningful, and usually more photogenic, when it occurs far from home. Some of the screen's most fondly remembered romances have been foreign affairs.*

# Pygmalion (1938)

# My Fair Lady (1963)

George Bernard Shaw's witty, biting Pygmalion is more than a modern retelling of the legend of a sculptor who fell in love with his own creation. In Shaw's play the sculptor is grammarian Henry Higgins, who grows fond of the cockney flower girl, Eliza Doolittle, whom he molds into a lady. It is also a social commentary, a paean to women's equality and one of the most reluctant love stories in theatrical history.

But it is the love story—or, rather, its characters' staunch denial of it—that provides the chemistry for both the 1938 *Pygmalion* and the Lerner and Loewe musical adapted from it in 1963, *My Fair Lady*.

In the original film a stern yet playful Leslie Howard, forty-eight, is the imperious Professor Higgins while Wendy Hiller—twenty-six and less angular than she'd be in a few years—is Eliza, the cockney lass who comes to him to learn how to be "a real lady" (which she pronounces "lie-dee"). Given the stiff Edwardian clothes, British reserve and chilly class distinctions that separate Higgins and Eliza, the fact that they fall undeniably in love is nothing short of amazing.

Or do they? In Shaw's play, Eliza walks out on Higgins rather than submit to his demand that, even though she is now a lady, she remain as his secretary—not his wife. Marriage never enters Higgins' misogynistic mind.

When producer Gabriel Pascal obtained the film rights to *Pygmalion*, Shaw himself wrote the script (and won an Oscar), appending the now-famous ending in which Eliza returns, only to find a smug Higgins who starts right back in ordering her about. The change was typically Shavian: although love had triumphed, it would have to be on equal terms—in effect, a happy ending that was neither happy nor an ending.

Lerner and Loewe included that ending in their musical, *My Fair Lady*, adding a swell of music to romanticize Shaw's hard-edged finish. Directing it for the screen, George Cukor—with Rex Harrison duplicating his stage role and Audrey Hepburn edging out Broadway's Julie Andrews in a controversial casting decision—kept the gloss high and the pace slow.

Viewers of both films can come away with quite different experiences. The two Higginses and the two Elizas make for distinctly different pairings. Howard and Hiller are quite the better match, with his acerbic tongue and her regal bearing instantly causing sparks. The feline Harrison—whose celebrated talk-singing of the great songs is a personal triumph—loses ground in his scenes with Hepburn, who is too much the gamine to be the kind of lady that Shaw had in mind. Hepburn looks great in Cecil Beaton's Oscar-winning costumes, but nowhere beneath those petticoats is the pair of pants Eliza has to be capable of wearing.

As befits a love story by G. B. Shaw, both *Pygmalion* and *My Fair Lady* are romances of thought, not deed. Perhaps that's because, as in the Greek legend, not only has Pygmalion fallen in love with his creation but his creation—unbeknownst to her—has fallen in love with him.

*Pygmalion DIRECTORS: Anthony Asquith and Leslie Howard WITH: Leslie Howard, Wendy Hiller, Wilfrid Lawson, David Tree*

*My Fair Lady DIRECTOR: George Cukor WITH: Rex Harrison, Audrey Hepburn, Wilfrid Hyde-White, Stanley Holloway*

# Ninotchka (1939)

Count Leon d'Algout (Melvyn Douglas) is sitting on the floor of his Paris apartment with his latest conquest, a strikingly lovely Russian diplomat. "Oh, Ninotchka—Ninotchka, surely you feel some slight symptom of the divine passion. A general warmth in the palm of your hands—a strange heaviness in your limbs. A burning of the lips that isn't thirst but something a thousand times more tantalizing, more exciting, than thirst?"

How can a woman respond to such poetic lovemaking? "You are very talkative," replies Nina Ivanovna Yakushova (Greta Garbo), who moments later will pronounce their passionate kiss as "restful."

Billed as the movie in which "Garbo Laughs," *Ninotchka* was one of the great films of 1939. The script (written by Charles Brackett, Billy Wilder, and Walter Reisch) focuses on the improbable romance between an aristocrat and a Communist, set against MGM's version of prewar Paris— "when a siren was a brunette and not an alarm," as the prologue reads.

Leon may be a nobleman, but he is a no-account count, serving as little more than a gigolo to Grand Duchess Swana (Ina Claire), a White Russian who lost her position and her jewels in the October Revolution. Indeed, his initial reason for wooing Ninotchka is to get back the Duchess's jewels, which Ninotchka and her delegation have come to Paris to sell.

Ninotchka is a humorless, dour commissar, who carries her own bags from the train because to have someone else do it would be a "social injustice." ("That depends on the tip," answers the porter.) Her defining moment is when she espies a fashionable hat and remarks, "How can such a civilization survive which permits their women to put things like that on their heads?"

Director Ernst Lubitsch, however, is more interested in love than politics. If Ninotchka will be won over by Western democracy (eventually buying and wearing the hat she mocked), Leon will have to give up his wastrel ways and learn to think of the welfare of others.

*Ninotchka* is less about opposites attracting than of people finding common ground. The most celebrated sequence is when Ninotchka chooses to dine at a working-class restaurant, where she orders raw beets and carrots. ("Madame," says the owner, "this is a restaurant, not a meadow.") Leon follows her in and attempts to win her over with witty banter and silly jokes.

He insists that she laugh, but she remains as glum and businesslike as ever. Finally he decides she has no sense of humor—"None whatsoever." With that, he leans back in his chair and falls to the floor. And Garbo, as Ninotchka, laughs and laughs, with such heart and feeling that ultimately even Leon must concede that she *does*, indeed, have a sense of humor.

While the film remains a popular and delightful romantic comedy, it is has taken on a curious importance in the film career of Garbo, who retired from the screen after making just one more film (1941's *Two Faced Woman*). Critic Richard Schickel wrote in an essay on Garbo that the movie for which she is best remembered is her least typical:

"Of all her movies, the only one that remains alive for us today, the only one that is not the property of her ever-dwindling cult, the only one we contemplate reseeing with pleasure or recommend to younger people with confidence is the movie in which she and her colleagues so artfully satirized her screen persona: *Ninotchka*."

Atypical it may be, but it is a lovely film for which to be remembered.

*DIRECTOR: Ernst Lubitsch WITH: Greta Garbo, Melvyn Douglas, Ina Claire, Sig Rumann, Felix Bressart, Bela Lugosi, George Tobias*

# The Quiet Man (1952)

People refer to "the John Wayne syndrome" when they mean a man who hides his emotions, but is there any more romantic film than the one that stars John Wayne and is called *The Quiet Man?*

Shot in Ireland (Counties Mayo and Galway) by John Ford, *The Quiet Man* brims with images of the Ould Sod idealized in Technicolor—the sort of film that brings back memories that never really existed. It follows the rocky romance of American ex-prize fighter Sean Thornton (Wayne) who has returned to the land of his parents to buy the cottage in which he was born; and Mary Kate, Danahar (Maureen O'Hara), who has the misfortune to be the housekeeper of her disagreeable brother (Victor McLaglen). When Sean, in typical Yank fashion, declares himself for Mary Kate, he is told that custom demands he court her in the proper manner—that is, under the watchful (if bloodshot) eyes of town matchmaker Barry Fitzgerald.

They soon wed, but brother "Red" Will Danahar refuses to free her dowry. Without it. Mary Kate does not consider herself truly married and refuses Thornton her conjugal bed. It takes a knock-down, drag-out "discussion" between the two men clear across the scenic Irish countryside to settle the score.

*The Quiet Man* has about as much to do with the real Ireland as *Manhattan* has to do with the real New York City. Its rolling hillsides of emerald grass, boisterous pubs, friendly clergy (priest Ward Bond and minister Arthur Shields) and cherubic townspeople are right out of director Ford's idealized past.

But the real fantasies are Wayne's bold, love-smitten Thornton and O'Hara's lusty, robust Mary Kate. The stormy day when he arrives home to find her sweeping out his cottage, then kisses her, her flaming red hair blowing in the wind, is a triumphant moment of passion, and it's a hard audience indeed that fails to cheer for their clinch.

It's a good thing *The Quiet Man* is so wholesome. With all the traditions that the people of Innisfree strictly observe, it's a wonder the village has a next generation. As much as she loves Wayne, O'Hara will not consent to be his wife without her brother's approval. Even though both of them know their hearts, matchmaker Fitzgerald must clear the arrangements. And with his own heart bruised (he wants the widow Tillane—Mildred Natwick) McLaglen won't release O'Hara's possessions. There is a code of honor and therefore a sense of pride in meeting it.

John Wayne at forty-five was just past his prime when he played Sean Thornton, but Maureen O'Hara at thirty-two was just entering hers. Their chemistry is powerful: Mary Kate's inviting glances at Sean may not have been classical acting, but the thought of them must have warmed many a night in his lonely cottage in County Mayo.

And speaking of images, the last one in *The Quiet Man* has lit fires under viewers for decades. Wayne is tilling their garden; O'Hara whispers something in his ear and together they race into the house. As critic Danny Peary pined in *Cult Movies 3*, "What any of us—Irish and non-Irish alike—wouldn't give to know exactly what Mary Kate has suggested to the man she loves."

*DIRECTOR: John Ford WITH: John Wayne, Maureen O'Hara, Victor McLaglen, Barry Fitzgerald, Ward Bond*

# Roman Holiday (1953)

There are times when you connect with someone and it is just wonderful, but nonetheless it wasn't meant to be. With its story of the improbable pairing of a reporter and a princess, *Roman Holiday* reminds us that we are as touched by the brief encounter as the full-fledged romance, if it is with the right person.

At first glance the movie seems a throwback to the screwball comedies of the 1930s. Like *It Happened One Night* (1934), it features a runaway evading her family and a reporter seeking a story, and like *Ninotchka* (1939), we have a romance between a representative of the aristocracy and one of "the people." Yet there the similarities end, for sometimes there are obstacles we choose *not* to overcome.

Princess Anne (Audrey Hepburn) is in Rome on a European good-will tour for her unidentified country when she decides she can't take the pressure and responsibility and runs off into the night. She is found by Joe Bradley (Gregory Peck), an American reporter who—when he finally recognizes her—realizes he has stumbled onto a great story. Over the course of twenty-four hours they have a series of adventures, culminating in their leaping into a river and swimming away from pursuing bodyguards. These shared experiences eventually spark romance.

At this point the parallel is closer to *The Philadelphia Story* (1940), in which another "princess" and another reporter think they have found love after a moonlight swim. As in that film, the two characters are changed by their brief romantic encounter but realize the impossibility of its continuing. Anne returns not only ready to resume her responsibilities but prepared to take control of them. And it is a wiser Joe Bradley who goes to see her at her press conference, where he and his photographer (Eddie Albert) quietly let her know that her day of freedom will remain their shared secret.

The key moment in their relationship may be when one of the reporters asks her which stop on her tour she most enjoyed. One of her advisers signals her that she is to give a canned answer about how much she enjoyed each of the cities. She begins to comply but then interrupts herself to say what she really feels. It was her Roman holiday that stands out. "I will cherish my visit here in memory as long as I live."

How like Rick Blaine (Humphrey Bogart) telling Ilsa Lund (Ingrid Bergman) in *Casablanca* (1942), "We'll always have Paris" as he sends her off on the plane with her husband. Some love affairs aren't meant to be for eternity, but they'll be treasured forever nonetheless.

Certainly one of the happiest memories for viewers of *Roman Holiday* is that it is "the movie that introduced Audrey Hepburn" as a star. (She had already had several film roles, including a bit in the 1951 British comedy *The Lavender Hill Mob*, but this was where she began to be noticed.) Her understated elegance mixed with innocence made her a beguiling star for years to come.

Hepburn's allure is clearest in the "mouth of truth" scene, in which Joe tells her the legend of a gigantic statue that bites off the hands of people who fail to tell the truth. He pretends that it has gotten him, and her shrieks of terror capture us for a moment. After several years of postwar cynicism, her naïveté is refreshing.

Peck provides the perfect counterpoint, readily understanding that this is Hepburn's film. In the final shot of the movie he waits to see whether Princess Anne has really departed or will come back to see him. When he realizes she has gone, he turns and leaves the ornate hall, with an expression that can only be read to mean that she is not the only one who will cherish her visit to Rome.

*Roman Holiday*, shot on location by William Wyler, offers ample proof that Rome and romance are closely linked.

*DIRECTOR: William Wyler WITH: Audrey Hepburn, Gregory Peck, Eddie Albert*

# South Pacific (1958)

The people who brought the smash stage musical *South Pacific* to the movies inherited a weighty responsibility. The story of lonely American troops and simple natives on a tropical island during World War II was a breakthrough in its presentation of atypical (for both Broadway and Hollywood) love stories. It focused on two interracial romances—one between the white Lieutenant Cable (John Kerr) and the Polynesian Liat (France Nuyen), and one between nurse Nellie Forbush (Mitzi Gaynor) and widower Emile de Becque (Rossano Brazzi), who had fathered children by a native girl.

In so doing, *South Pacific* taunted those who demanded that the stage and screen reflect "traditional values" (a frequent catchphrase for racism). By setting it all against the seductive backdrop of the south seas during the turbulent period of World War II, the creators were making the point that when the whole world no longer makes sense, neither do narrowminded visions of what love should be.

The stage and film versions of *South Pacific* also show this torn allegiance. On the one hand, the movie stuck to its guns in making a strong—and early—plea for tolerance. On the other, however, it stumbled a bit as a movie when the filmmakers tried to achieve emotional effects by applying theatrical techniques: colored filters, painted backdrops (though perhaps not on purpose), proscenium staging and self-conscious pauses after musical numbers to allow for imagined applause.

Joshua Logan, who had directed *South Pacific* to immense acclaim on Broadway (and who later filmed the musicals *Camelot* and *Paint Your Wagon*), proved to be as stodgy in his screen career as he was brilliant on the stage.

Yet *South Pacific*'s importance is assured. Its breaking of racial barriers, an element that distinguished James A. Michener's source novella, was preserved against considerable opposition.

"What we were saying was said through Nellie," recalled the show's composer, Richard Rodgers. "'All that is piffle.' Prejudice falls away in front of something that's really important."

The "Madame Butterfly" syndrome—love forbidden by racism and ignorance—has long sullied Hollywood's treatment of interracial romance. For every *A Patch of Blue* (1965), *Guess Who's Coming to Dinner* (1967), or even *100 Rifles* (1969), there are far more instances where "exotic" characters (black, Asian, Native American, etc.) are portrayed by whites wearing makeup: *Duel in the Sun*, *Love is a Many-Splendored Thing*, *Pinky*, *Showboat*, *Stay Away Joe*, *The King and I*, etc.

The enduring strength of these "forbidden loves" inspired *South Pacific* to reach for emotional heights. Emile's and Nellie's "Twin Soliloquies" and their "Some Enchanted Evening" finale are undeniably moving; Cable's "Younger Than Springtime," sung to Liat, is an affirmation of love's triumph over prejudice; so is his angry, "You've Got to Be Carefully Taught," which lists the ways people are ritually raised to hate others. These are exquisite, private moments shared by people torn between the world at large and the anguish they feel within.

It is ironic that *South Pacific*, which is set during a war against oppression, should concern itself with oppression set against a war. Its universal themes and eternal truths overcome any reservations. Like the mystical island of Bali H'ai that tempts the sailors, *South Pacific* tempts audiences to pine for something that is as far away as perfection yet as close as the desire to attain it.

*DIRECTOR: Joshua Logan WITH: Rossano Brazzi, Mitzi Gaynor, John Kerr, France Nuyen*

# Gigi (1958)

**M**arriage is not forbidden to us," Gigi (Leslie Caron) is told by her Aunt Alicia (Isabel Jeans), "but instead of getting married at once, it sometimes happens we get married at last."

In this musical adaptation of Colette's novel (words and music by the *My Fair Lady* team of Alan Jay Lerner and Frederick Loewe), Gigi is a young girl on the verge of womanhood in turn-of-the-century Paris. She lives with her Grandmama (Hermione Gingold) preparing for the only sort of life a poor but well-bred woman can hope for: that of paramour to wealthy men. Her aunt teaches her how to dine on delicacies and how to tell a genuine pearl necklace from those that are only "dipped," but doesn't prepare her for the unexpected: love.

Gaston Lachailles (Louis Jourdan) is part of that high society but has lost interest in the nightclubs, the gossip and the women who are more interested in collecting jewels than in romance. His one joy is visiting Grandmama, where he plays cards with Gigi (who insists she doesn't *have* to cheat to beat him) and sees how much pleasure grandmother and granddaughter take in things that have long since palled for his jaded tastes.

When Grandmama insists that Gaston accept Gigi as a woman and not merely as a schoolgirl, he is stunned. In a musical soliloquy, lushly directed by Vincente Minnelli, he finally admits to himself that she has been "growing up before my eyes." Unfortunately, Grandmama and Aunt Alicia have been doing their best to fit Gigi into the life that Gaston has already sung is "a bore!"

By this point, Gigi has considered the sort of shallow life they might lead and has decided it "won't do." Their night on the town turns out to be an unhappy experience for both of them. The sophistication that has been the subject of all her lessons has smothered the *joie de vivre* that attracted Gaston to Gigi in the first place. Instead of the girl who is giddy at the prospect of a sip of wine ("The Night They Invented Champagne"), she is now a woman who is pouring Gaston's coffee and selecting his cigars.

Her attitude is ironic in light of the youthful rebellion against adult standards that would begin just a few years after the 1958 release of *Gigi*. Her temperament is the mirror image of those who led the sixties revolt against middle-class values: she rejects a life of serial love affairs and insists on commitment and marriage.

In the course of the film we get an idea of both lifestyles, and our sympathies are with Gigi, no matter how beautiful they all look in their period costumes (designed by Cecil Beaton, who won one of the film's nine Oscars). Maurice Chevalier, as Gaston's aging Uncle Honoré, may enjoy a life free from obligation, but he seems wistful about what might have been when reminiscing with Grandmama about *their* love affair ("I Remember It Well"). Later, he is visibly relieved as he sings about how "comfortable" he is now that the foibles of young love are behind him ("I'm Glad I'm Not Young Any More").

Gaston and Grandmama realize that Gigi is right. If love is to be worth having, it's got to be worth preserving as well. When Gaston asks for Gigi's hand in marriage, Grandmama can only say, "Thank heaven," the cue for Honoré to reprise "Thank Heaven for Little Girls" and for us to depart this Technicolor Paris of romance and music.

Not all the great musicals have aged well, but "Gigi" is as sparkling today as it was when it won a bevy of Oscars including Best Picture, Best Director and Best Screenplay. Years later it was adapted for the stage—reversing the usual process—but it's hard not to see this one as it was originally conceived for the screen.

Ah yes, we remember it well.

*DIRECTOR: Vincente Minnelli WITH: Leslie Caron, Louis Jourdan, Maurice Chevalier, Hermione Gingold, Isabel Jeans, Eva Gabor*

# Doctor Zhivago (1965)

For nearly three decades moviegoers have fallen under the spell of *Doctor Zhivago*. Charmed by its snowy vistas, sighing with its secret lovers or humming along with "Lara's Theme" they are caught in the sweep of the Russian Revolution and the travails of its complex characters. It hardly matters that nobody who shot the film has anything to do with Russia: *Zhivago* is a rousing love story whatever its authenticity.

No literature is more passionate than that of Russia, yet the best-known Russian cinema has generally been cold and formal, the result perhaps of having to exist within a Communist system. Even the work of the great masters Sergei Eisenstein (*October, Battleship Potemkin*) and Vsevoloá Puduvkin (*Mother*) gets more excitement from crowds than individuals, a factor perhaps of the Bolshevik mandate that the Soviet state was better served by propaganda than escapism.

That is why, to everybody's chagrin, Boris Pasternak's sweeping novel *Doctor Zhivago*—and director David Lean's equally sweeping film of it—are thought of as being typically Russian. Neither is, but for different reasons; Lean's American-Italian coproduction was shot largely in Spain and England, and Pasternak's book was banned by the Kremlin for daring to suggest that Communism was flawed. But if *Doctor Zhivago* is not Russian in pedigree, it surely is in spirit. The sprawling story of the adulterous romance between an aristocratic doctor-poet (Omar Sharif) and a young revolutionary woman (Julie Christie) offered the meticulous Lean an immense canvas on which to play out, as the ads promised, "a love caught in the fire of revolution." Surely its grand panoramas, swirling snowstorms, glistening photography, thundering armies, and impeccable production design offered enough heat to melt even a heart frozen in Siberia. With Maurice Jarre's haunting "Lara's Theme" (rechristened "Somewhere My Love" for its innumerable cover versions), *Doctor Zhivago* is that rare thing—an intimate spectacle.

Unfortunately, the critics didn't think so in 1965 and their pans nearly doomed the film to early withdrawal, despite its high-visibility road-show release. Lean credits MGM's stalwart support and Jarre's music with turning *Doctor Zhivago* around into the most profitable film he ever made.

It is also his most romantic. Who can forget the meeting of Sharif and Christie aboard a trolley—they accidentally brush shoulders and we cut to the tram's antenna sparking on its overhead wire. Or a virginal Christie returning home and meeting the lecherous bureaucrat Komarovsky (Rod Steiger), who has just had his way with her mother.

"How old are you?" he asks.

"Seventeen," she says meekly. As he undresses her with his eyes, then smirks, the sexual tension is palpable.

So are the moments when Sharif, as a field doctor during the civil war, remains faithful to his Moscow-bound wife (Geraldine Chaplin) despite being tempted by Christie, who is his nurse. When Christie and Sharif finally consummate their love—taking it across the steppes and into hiding in a crystalline winter home—*Doctor Zhivago* succeeds, as do they, in keeping the real world at bay.

Although it diminishes the events of 1917 as "a grand romantic era giving way to a new and violent order" (as another ad line glibly, if naïvely, put it), *Doctor Zhivago* has since earned a place not as a lesson in politics but as one of the screen's most fondly remembered affairs of the heart.

*DIRECTOR: David Lean WITH: Omar Sharif, Julie Christie, Rod Steiger, Geraldine Chaplin*

# Mahogany (1975)

*M*ahogany has all the ingredients of a world-class romantic movie: colorful locations, fabulous costumes, beautiful actors and a passionate story. It doesn't succeed in that last category, but in reaching for the skies it earned a place in movie history as the one film that treated Diana Ross as a Hollywood star.

By any measure, Ross should have been one of the movies' greatest romantic leading actresses. In 1972, already a well-established Motown recording star, she crossed over to movies with *Lady Sings the Blues* in which she won acclaim as the tragic singer Billie Holiday.

Given a color-blind Hollywood, she would have immediately had another film built around her by a studio eager to exploit her talent and box office appeal. But the industry was still mourning the dwindling receipts from the crude "blaxpoitation" pictures it had churned out during the early 1970s and virtually abandoned the one *bona fide* black female star the decade had produced.

Instead, Ross and Motown's fiercely possessive president, Berry Gordy, spent three years entangled in what became *Mahogany*, an uneasy blend of political savvy and Hollywood convention. Ross plays a poor girl who, on the way to triumph as a fashion designer, is discovered by photographer Anthony Perkins and becomes a top European model. All the while her lover, Detroit lawyer/political activist Billy Dee Williams, fails as she succeeds. They want each other but must pursue their separate goals; in the end, despite her success, she chucks it all and comes home to stand by him on election eve.

Famous chiefly for its Oscar-nominated song, "Do You Know Where You're Going To?," *Mahogany* is also notable as a showcase for clothes (which Ross designed) and a forum for commentary (visiting Ross in Rome, Williams wryly notes, "Here they call them ruins; back home they call them slums").

Yet the power behind the films endurance comes from the reunion of Ross and Williams, her *Lady* co-star. Condescendingly labeled "the black Clark Gable" by the press at the time, Williams adds charismatic, superbly controlled ice to Ross' fire; as a screen couple they swap sermons, kisses, tantrums and quips. Although the script by John Byrum and the direction by Gordy (who replaced Byrum as director midway through production) don't fully realize the material, there is an undeniable sparkle to the Ross-Williams scenes.

Compare their special chemistry with the others: Ross and Anthony Perkins, then Ross and Jean-Pierre Aumont. Perkins, as an asexual photographer, names his discoveries after inanimate objects (hence, "Mahogany"). When they dutifully go to bed together he cannot perform. Though this lets her (and the filmmakers) off the inter-racial hook, it hastens the end of their mentor-protege relationship.

Her dealings with Aumont are even more juvenile: he's a wealthy businessman who sets her up in the clothing business, lets her live in his villa in Rome, worships the designer shoes she walks on, yet never asks about collecting sexual favors until it's too late. Ross' naivete with both men is staggering, but it serves to make one want to see her back with Williams as soon as the plot—and the characters' unyielding egos—will allow.

The years since *Lady Sings the Blues* and *Mahogany* may have produced more African-American movie stars (Eddie Murphy, Whoopi Goldberg, Margaret Avery, Denzel Washington, Lonette McKee, Danny Glover, Wesley Snipes, Morgan Freeman) but none who expanded and sensitized the screen like Ross and Williams. Their loss is ours, too.

*DIRECTOR: Berry Gordy WITH: Diana Ross, Billy Dee Williams, Anthony Perkins*

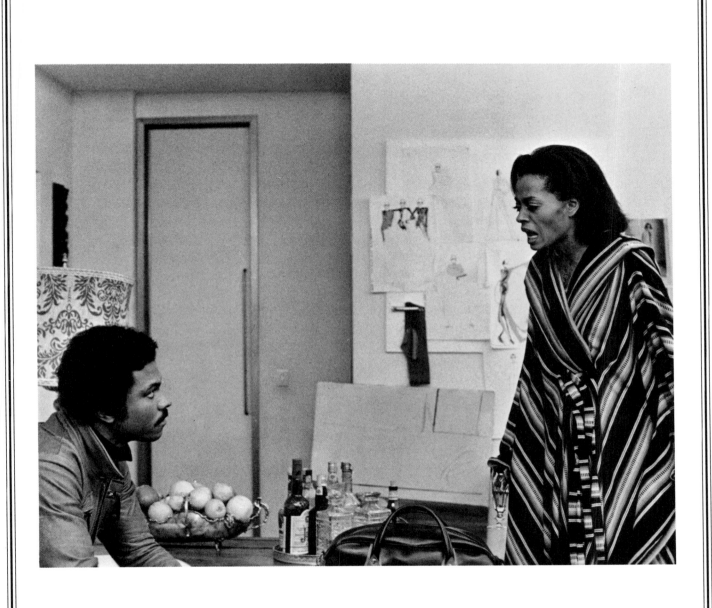

47

# The Year of Living Dangerously (1982)

There are times when life seems especially vivid and people live for the moment, none more so than when two lovers meet against the background of imminent war. There's no time for games or subtlety. When you can't be sure what will happen from one minute to the next, you take risks that you might ordinarily shun.

Such is the situation for Guy Hamilton (Mel Gibson) when he arrives in Indonesia in 1965. He's a correspondent for the Australian Broadcasting System, there to report the expected civil war between the left-wing government and the right-wing military. Befriended by the diminutive photographer Billy Kwan (Oscar winner Linda Hunt in a man's role), Guy is introduced not only to murky Third World politics but to the stunning Jill Bryant (Sigourney Weaver). Jill is only weeks away from ending a tour of duty at the British Embassy.

Billy, who keeps files on everyone he knows, is as much in love with Jill as every other man who meets her. "I asked her to marry me once," he confesses to Guy. "She turned me down." Instead, Billy lives for his friendships. He makes a point of introducing Guy and Jill, in hopes of living vicariously through them.

Jill is not looking for any new attachments, since she's counting the days to her departure. Yet when Guy and Jill look at each other it is lust at first sight. They practically devour each other with their eyes. She tries to put him off, but with the clock inexorably ticking, she doesn't really want to.

He arrives at an embassy party just before curfew and spirits her away; the danger of getting caught is part of the allure. They race through a road block, braving a fusillade of bullets, and are so exhilarated by the experience that it's all they can do to keep driving on. While they tryst at Billy's bungalow, Billy comes out and sensuously fingers the bullet holes in the car. He *does* understand them, because he has the same feelings, which remain largely unexpressed.

The press of time and the political situation give Guy and Jill's romance its tang, but are also what almost tears them apart. Jill learns of an arms shipment coming into the country and tells Guy so that he can flee the country before war breaks out. Is he her lover or a journalist? He chooses to play the reporter and suddenly, they're not quite on the same side anymore.

Guy gets his story but realizes in the process that this is not his world. After Billy's senseless death, the violence no longer serves as an aphrodisiac. He defies the odds and makes it to Jill's plane in time to join her in escape. Our final image is of their embrace. But do they have any future together?

Director Peter Weir, working on the script he wrote with David William and C. J. Koch (based on Koch's novel), doesn't try to answer that question. Instead he focuses on the atmosphere where reporters fulfill their conflicting needs for danger and comfort, and where foreigners try not to be touched by the images of crushing poverty all around them.

Yet one has to wonder what Guy and Jill will have in common once they're back in her London or his Sydney. Like a shipboard romance, it may be that their encounter is defined by a particular time and a particular place. They may always remember each other; indeed, each may recall the other with a passion that others will compete against in vain. Yet one suspects that they themselves will be unable to live up to those memories of the times they spent "living dangerously."

*DIRECTOR: Peter Weir WITH: Mel Gibson, Sigourney Weaver, Linda Hunt, Michael Murphy*

# CHAPTER THREE

# Isn't It Romantic

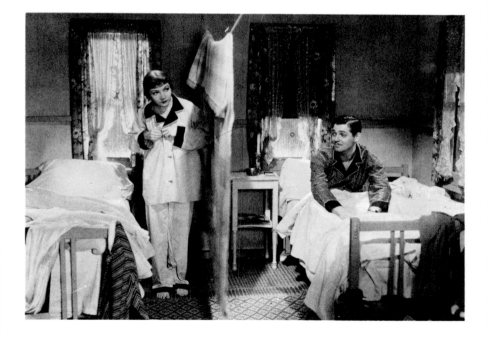

*The excitement of real love seldom meets the delicious standards of "reel" love, but it's always nice to try. People who wish for romance to be "just like in the movies" usually have one of the movies in mind.*

# The Gay Divorcee (1934)

In the world of romantic musical comedy there is Astaire and Rogers, and then there is everyone else. In the 1930s they were the premiere musical comedy team, so associated with each other that when their series of films ended it seemed as if an era had drawn to a close. And indeed it had.

First paired in 1933 in RKO's *Flying Down to Rio*, their presence remains the chief attraction of this otherwise forgettable film. Modern viewers of *Rio* are often surprised to find Astaire and Rogers billed fourth and fifth in the credits. No one was more surprised at their instant acclaim than RKO, which quickly decided to make them the focus of their own film. They would do eight more films together at the studio and a reunion film (*The Barkleys of Broadway*) at MGM a decade later.

Many of the elements for the Astaire-Rogers films were set in place with *The Gay Divorcee*. The frothy plot has Guy Holden (Astaire) fall instantly in love with Mimi Glossop (Rogers) when he sees her at a British customs station. Through a mix-up in identity, she believes him to be a professional co-respondent—a man hired to "compromise" a woman so that her husband will be forced to divorce her. As always, their problem is how can they get beyond the mix-up to a real romance.

In the world of an Astaire-Rogers film, there is only one suitable time for romance, and that is while dancing. In the only Cole Porter song to survive the transition from stage to screen, Astaire professes his love for Rogers "Night and Day." What follows is a dance sequence that transforms the characters from comical combatants to lovers. First Astaire is a supplicant, pleading with Rogers to remain and dance. She allows herself to be convinced and, hesitantly at first, joins in. Finally, they dance together in a joyful celebration as the music builds and they twirl around cheek to cheek. Commentators on their films, such as Arlene Croce and John Mueller, have noted that the whole number is one of seduction and consummation. Indeed, at the conclusion of the dance Rogers sits languidly on a couch and Astaire offers, "Cigarette?"

There is also a lavish production number for "The Continental," which only pales in comparison to the even more surreal concoctions that Busby Berkeley was creating over at Warner Bros. for films like *42nd Street* and *Footlight Parade*. "The Continental" won the Oscar for Best Song that year, the first time that category was included.

Interestingly, the reason the number was included at all was that the Astaire-Rogers production number from *Flying Down to Rio*—called the Carioca—had inexplicably set off a national dance craze. Indeed, the original ads for *The Gay Divorcee* dubbed its stars "The King and Queen of the Carioca." This tactic would be tried once more the following year in *Top Hat* with "The Piccolino" which failed to live up to the success of its predecessor.

The conventional wisdom on why the Astaire-Rogers team worked so wonderfully is that "he gave her class and she gave him sex"—he polished up her image and she made him seem attractive. Yet that really doesn't do their films justice. Aside from the fanciful art deco designs of RKO production designer Van Nest Polglase and music from people like Cole Porter, Irving Berlin and Jerome Kern, it is those incredible dance numbers that leave viewers feeling as if the law of gravity has temporarily been repealed which remain strongest in our memories.

*DIRECTOR: Mark Sandrich WITH: Fred Astaire, Ginger Rogers, Edward Everett Horton, Alice Brady, Eric Blore, Erik Rhodes*

# It Happened One Night (1934)

Can true love blossom when two totally different people are thrown together by chance and forced to work together? *It Happened One Night* answers with a resounding yes, and audiences agreed, setting off a cycle of films that would last until World War II.

Spoiled heiress Ellie Andrews (Claudette Colbert) is fleeing from her father (Walter Connolly), who is trying to get her spur-of-the-moment marriage annulled. She goes off unaided to wend her way back to her husband, a man she barely knows. Along the way she will learn that in Depression-era America not everyone enjoyed indoor plumbing, and that no matter how politely you ask, a bus driver will not wait while you run a few personal errands.

Early on, she meets Peter Warne (Clark Gable), a hard-living reporter who has just been fired from his New York newspaper. He recognizes her and offers her a deal: he'll help her get back to King Wesley (Jameson Thomas), her aviator/playboy husband, if she'll give him the exclusive story. Thus starts a comic adventure that will be based on their equal partnership and will end with her dumping King at the altar to run off with Peter.

Director Frank Capra and writer Robert Riskin helped establish the "screwball" romances of the 1930s by letting the romantic leads handle the comedy instead of casting established comedians. These movies inevitably focus on two characters who cause each other to change, falling in love in the process.

Ellie, who has lived in the cocoon of vast wealth, needs to experience life and see that she can actually take care of herself. Peter, who has never cared for anything beyond his next story and his next drink, not only needs to care about someone else, he also has to learn that he is not entirely self-sufficient. Nowhere is this more apparent than when the two are out hitchhiking and he is lecturing on the different thumb gestures and how they work.

"I'm gonna write a book about it," he tells her. When car after car speeds by, Ellie is emboldened to try *her* method: pulling up a skirt and showing off her shapely leg. The next car screeches to a stop, and Peter mutters in defeat, "Why didn't you take *all* your clothes off? You could have stopped forty cars."

"I'll remember that when we need forty cars," she says with a smile.

Ironically, this classic comedy was initially looked at as punishment by its two stars, who didn't know they were making movie history. Being loaned to Columbia Pictures—then a "Poverty Row" operation—was like asking the President of the United States if he'd mind being a county commissioner for a few weeks. For Gable it literally was a punishment, as his bosses at MGM felt it was time to reassert their authority. For Colbert, a star at Paramount, it meant taking a role already turned down by Miriam Hopkins, Margaret Sullavan and Myrna Loy. She initially said no.

Yet the finished film enhanced the careers of virtually everyone associated with it, becoming one of only two pictures in history to win all five top Oscars: Best Picture, Best Director, Best Screenplay, Best Actor, Best Actress. (The other one was *One Flew Over the Cuckoo's Nest*.)

Audiences still cheer when Mr. Andrews tells Ellie she can get out of the wedding to the wrong man and that a getaway car is waiting to take her to Peter. *It Happened One Night* worked its Hollywood magic on everyone it touched, and the magic continues to this day.

*DIRECTOR: Frank Capra WITH: Clark Gable, Claudette Colbert, Walter Connolly, Roscoe Karns, Alan Hale*

# Love Affair (1939)

# An Affair to Remember (1957)

Other than *Casablanca*, no movie is more certain to get people to stay home and watch TV than Leo McCarey's 1957 charmer, *An Affair to Remember*, a romantic comedy that turns serious.

Cary Grant and Deborah Kerr meet aboard a cruise ship, pledge their love, and plan to wed as soon as they hit land and ditch their respective fiances. They agree to meet atop the Empire State Building if—and only if—each is free and still wants to marry. Hurrying to keep the assignation, Kerr is struck by a car and paralyzed. Grant, however, wrongly assumes she demurred and leaves, shattered. Still loving him, Kerr moves away and never tells Grant about her injury, preferring to keep the memory of their affair alive. When he happens to discover her secret (on Christmas Eve) he renews his promise to marry her, and together they face her disability.

It's hard not to like the skillful interplay between the worldly Nicky Ferrante (Grant) and the equally spirited Terry McKay (Kerr). At first they seem only a movie match, suited only because they can swap quips and model dazzling fashions. But then we learn—during a moving visit to Grant's aged grandmother (Cathleen Nesbitt)—of deeper emotional capacities. This odd detour in a comedy sets the stage for what will follow. Director McCarey (*The Awful Truth*, *Going My Way*) was a past master at building and milking gags, cajoling actors to achieve an ease of style, and shamelessly dropping nuggets of sentimentality into fertile fields of comedy. Remarkably, McCarey had already done it better eighteen years earlier in his first version of this same story, *Love Affair*, whose script won an Oscar in 1939.

In the original, Charles Boyer is a French rake, Michel Marnay, while Irene Dunne is the feisty Terry McKay. Because Boyer's gifts lay more in charm than comedy, McCarey wisely made him Dunne's foil, but never so obviously that the integrity of either character was compromised. They were simply two adults having a wonderful time, and the audience shared it.

The final intimate exchange in which Boyer/Grant and Dunne/Kerr reconcile is intricately written (by Delmer Daves and Donald Ogden Stewart) and brilliantly carried off. In a sense, the first version was a rehearsal for the remake. Here's what's at stake: Boyer gallantly pretends to have missed their Empire State Building reunion knowing that it was Dunne who failed to show, but not knowing why. Dunne has to free Boyer of her, also never telling him why. Both must obviously lie that each has gotten over the affair. And finally Boyer must discover the truth and convince Dunne that it makes no difference to their love. Both films do it well; the first does it better.

When a financially strapped McCarey remade RKO's *Love Affair* for Twentieth Century-Fox as *An Affair to Remember*, an arrangement was made with RKO to withdraw their original from circulation. What a pity that the only version most people now know is the remake.

Boyer's character is more textured; for instance, on board the cruise ship he insults four girls who demand his autograph and almost decks a bratty kid for being precocious. Grant, opting to be likable instead of vain like Boyer, merely walks away from people who have already shown the audience how obnoxious they are. In other words, Boyer is tamed by an exceptional woman while Grant is merely being polite to a well-bred lady. In Irene Dunne the movies had a uniquely gifted star who could easily appear in comedies, dramas, musicals—and sometimes combine all the elements into one. Either way, though, this story of unqualified love is a moving and enduring memory.

*Love Affair*: DIRECTOR: Leo McCarey WITH: Charles Boyer, Deborah Kerr, Maria Ouspenskaya

*An Affair to Remember*: DIRECTOR: Leo McCarey WITH: Cary Grant, Irene Dunne, Cathleen Nesbitt

# Holiday (1938)

One of the lessons of romantic comedies is that the two people constituting the couple have to be on the same wavelength. In *Holiday*, Johnny Case (Cary Grant) finds his ideal woman, someone who will share his zest for life. Unfortunately for him, it is his fiancée's sister.

Johnny is a young man with a mission: make a lot of money young and then go on an extended vacation. But Johnny is no pre–World War II yuppie. Having worked his way from poverty into investment banking, he wants time to find himself. "I've been working since I was 10—I want to find out why I've been working."

On a brief holiday ski trip he meets the lovely Julia Seton (Doris Nolan), who he thinks will be "the perfect playmate." Nevertheless in Philip Barry's play, and in this adaptation by George Cukor and screenwriter Donald Ogden Stewart, what Julia really wants to do is talk Johnny out of these silly notions and get him down to the serious work of making a lot of money, as her family has always done.

Johnny arrives at the delivery entrance of the Seton mansion assuming it must be Julia's place of employment. There he meets the rest of her family: her humorless father (Henry Kolker), her alcoholic brother (Lew Ayres in a touching performance) and the black sheep of the family, sister Linda (Katharine Hepburn). Linda loathes the family's lifestyle and their household. Her hangout is a family playroom up on the third floor that was decorated by her late mother.

The audience is way ahead of the characters here, for we all know that Johnny and Linda will be together by the end of the film. What's fascinating in this wonderful comedy about following your heart are the alternative role models Johnny has to choose from in imagining his future life.

Quite apart from the father, the lavish New Year's engagement party (which Linda had hoped to throw for just a small gathering of friends) provides a stark contrast between two married couples who are among the guests. Seton and Laura Cram (Henry Daniell, Binnie Barnes) are shallow and unhappy, cheerfully greeting the other guests while snidely talking behind their backs. Linda calls them "the Witch and Dopey" when they show up in the playroom.

Providing a delightful contrast are Susan and Nick Potter (Jean Dixon, Edward Everett Horton), college professors who are Johnny's closest friends. Their playfulness together goes from witty exchanges to putting on a Punch and Judy show for Linda and her brother. "There's not a lot of people like Nick," says Susan with real affection. (Apparently not. Horton had played the same role in the previous 1930 film version.)

That idea of playfulness is ultimately what separates Julia and Johnny and gives Linda her shot at happiness. It's an awkward triangle, with Linda not really wanting to compete with her sister. She tries everything she can to keep them together, but Nick suggests to her, "Isn't it just possible that the things we like in Johnny may be the very things that your sister can't stand? And the fate that you feel that he'll save her from may be the one fate in the whole world that she really wants?"

Ultimately Johnny is doubtful but agrees to give Julia's way a trial run, but when her father starts planning a honeymoon that will include studies of European banking ("There's no harm in combining a little business with pleasure, is there?"), Johnny breaks it off and heads off on an ocean cruise with Nick and Susan.

In one of the great romantic clinches, Johnny is doing his trademark backflip in the hallway of the ocean liner when Linda appears while he is in mid-flip. As he falls to the floor, she kneels down to join him and we know that Johnny has found his "perfect playmate" at last.

*DIRECTOR: George Cukor WITH: Cary Grant, Katharine Hepburn, Lew Ayres, Henry Kolker, Doris Nolan, Jean Dixon, Edward Everett Horton, Henry Daniell, Binnie Barnes*

# Intermezzo (1939)

Two lovers are strolling among ruins in a Mediterranean village. Carved on a stone are the words "Mon amour dure apres la mort" ("My love endures after death"). Holger Brandt (Leslie Howard) turns to Anita Hoffman (Ingrid Bergman) and says, "That was written for us, and for everyone on earth who will ever feel as we do now."

Holger and Anita's love cannot last, and audiences knew this even as they went to see what critic Leonard Maltin has called "one of the best love stories ever filmed." For in running off to their romantic hideaway on the Mediterranean, they are both cutting off the rest of their lives. Holger is a famous concert violinist from Sweden with a wife and two children. Anita was his daughter's piano tutor and was herself studying to be a classical pianist. She ends up involved with Holger and has to drop her studies as he is forced to abandon his family.

Anita tries to break it off. "All along I've been hating this kind of thing, always meeting like this, in out-of-the-way places, little dark corners, sneaking about in fear of being seen," she argues, telling him that it makes no sense to continue.

"Love isn't sensible," he answers. Thus they go off on what she later describes as an "intermezzo"—a short passage between the major sections of an extended musical work. When she wins an important scholarship, and sees how much Holger misses his children, she decides to be the strong one and break it off. "We know in our hearts that love like ours is wrong," she writes him, and they never see each other again. Meanwhile Holger must melodramatically suffer a while longer (including being the cause of a near fatal accident involving his daughter) before his wife finally can say, "Welcome home."

In many ways, *Intermezzo* was a "welcome" for Ingrid Bergman, who had been acting in Sweden and had appeared in the original Swedish version of the film. She was "introduced" to American audiences in 1939 with this David O. Selznick production, and in typical Selznick fashion he agonized over her height, her name, how she would photograph on film, and how boring she sounded in interviews when she mentioned that she was married to a dentist.

Selznick also wondered whether audiences would understand what the musical term *intermezzo* meant and considered renaming it *Love Story* thirty-one years before Ali MacGraw called Ryan O'Neal a "preppie." Eventually the film was titled *Intermezzo: A Love Story.*

For Leslie Howard, making *Intermezzo* was a delicious irony. In his book *Memo from: David O. Selznick*, Rudy Behlmer reprints correspondence in which Selznick tries to undercut Howard's bargaining position by pointing out how several of his recent films had flopped. In the end, though, Selznick had to make Howard associate producer on *Intermezzo* (a film the actor *wanted* to make) in order to get him to play the bland Ashley Wilkes in *Gone With the Wind* (a part he disliked).

Near the end of his life, Selznick was annoyed that he might be remembered for *Gone With the Wind* and not for any subsequent films, and he tried several times to make movies that he thought would rival his greatest success. In 1960 he attempted to raise interest in a remake of *Intermezzo*, which he envisaged in the then current style of a lavish soap opera shot in color on actual European locations.

It was never to be, but it's interesting to note one casting idea Selznick had for the remake. He thought conductor Leonard Bernstein might be perfect for Holger, since they wouldn't have to fake the music and Bernstein "is as much an actor as he is a musician."

*DIRECTOR: Gregory Ratoff WITH: Leslie Howard, Ingrid Bergman, Edna Best, Cecil Kellaway, John Halliday*

# The More the Merrier (1943)

One of the recurring conventions of the romantic comedy is that the audience often knows before the characters do that they belong together. The audience usually figures out from the opening credits who will end up with whom. In *The More the Merrier* we know that when Mr. Dingle (Charles Coburn) sublets half of the half-apartment he has himself sublet, it is simply so that his new roommate can meet his "landlady."

The comedy comes from the fact that the landlady, Connie Milligan (Jean Arthur), spends most of the film insisting that she is in love with Mr. Pendergast (Richard Gaines), whom she never addresses by his first name in spite of the fact that they've been engaged for twenty-two months. She's fated to end up with Joe Carter (Joel McCrea), but it takes Dingle a tremendous amount of meddling to pull it off.

*The More the Merrier* bridges the gap between the prewar screwball comedies and the increasingly domestic stories that would come after. Here Connie flees commitment through her pseudo-relationship with Mr. Pendergast. There's no passion there, and her highest praise for him is that, at forty-two, he has reached "a very safe, sane age." Joe, on the other hand, has played the field but has never wanted to settle down.

In an earlier time this couple would have made a cross-country trip or chased a leopard or fought City Hall together and, in that manner, found true love. World War II was now raging, however, and priorities were different (director Stevens left Hollywood soon after completing the picture to join the Army Signal Corps' film unit along with such fellow directors as Frank Capra and John Huston).

Connie works in Washington, D.C., and decides to do her patriotic duty to relieve the tremendous overcrowding in the city by subletting part of her apartment. Joe is a military man due to leave shortly on a top-secret mission. By 1943 even comedic romances are being touched by the war, and happy endings are sometimes postponed for the duration.

Enter Dingle. He's a Congressional consultant whose motto is taken from Admiral Farragut: "Damn the torpedoes, full speed ahead." Needing a place to stay, he dismisses the other applicants for Connie's space and then convinces her to let it to him, against her own wishes. He then finds Joe and agrees to share *his* space with him.

If the audience weren't on the side of romance, Dingle's interference would be downright obnoxious. He reads Connie's diary, keeps Pendergast busy so that Joe will have to walk her home, and then denies everything to make Pendergast think Connie has been sharing more than surplus housing with Joe. Dingle is really more of a fairy godfather, however, acting in the other characters' best interests and bringing them together the way *we* want them to be. Coburn is so endearing in the role he won a well-deserved Supporting Actor Oscar that year for his performance.

The final touch is something that could only work in the movies. Connie and Joe have been sleeping side by side, separated only by a thin wall. Now after a rushed marriage (to avoid a possible scandal) they are in their separate rooms, wondering if they'll ever see each other after he departs the next day on his secret mission. But director George Stevens parks his camera outside the building as Joe opens the row of windows in his room. Suddenly we notice that he is opening the windows in *her* room. Dingle—in one final bit of meddling—has had the wall between them torn down.

When the film was remade in 1966 as *Walk, Don't Run* the setting was shifted from wartime Washington to the 1964 Tokyo Olympics. One other interesting shift: the role of the older meddler went to that star of so many romantic comedies Cary Grant, in what was to be his final film.

*DIRECTOR: George Stevens WITH: Jean Arthur, Joel McCrea, Charles Coburn, Richard Gaines*

# Breakfast at Tiffany's (1961)

Avoiding responsibility may seem like a nice way to live one's life, at least for a little while, but as Holly Golightly (Audrey Hepburn) and Paul Varjak (George Peppard) learn, it's no way to fall in love. By helping each other overcome the problems they cannot deal with on their own, they eventually gain control over their own lives.

It's interesting to ask why people still respond to Holly Golightly after more than three decades. While she's young and attractive, a moment's consideration shows she has very little to recommend her:

• She's inconsiderate: When we first meet her she is waking up her neighbor (Mickey Rooney) to buzz her into the building. She lost her key months before and can't be bothered to get it replaced, because she'd only lose it again.

• She's rude: When Paul moves into the building, she spies on him through his window and pries into his relationship with his "decorator" (Patricia Neal). She decides that Paul reminds her of her brother Fred and calls him by that name instead.

• She's a hypocrite: When Paul questions her about her life, she leaves in a huff, telling him, "If we're going to be friends, let's get one thing straight: I hate snoops."

• She's disloyal: She's walked out on one marriage (to Buddy Ebsen), and in the course of the story cavalierly dismisses several boyfriends and even her cat, whom she refuses to name for fear that it might mean she was responsible for it.

• She's impulsive: The night before a Hollywood screen test that her friend O.J. (Martin Balsam) has spent the better part of a year preparing her for, she skips town and heads East because she's "never been to New York before."

In spite of—or perhaps because of—her flaws, she brings out the protector in Paul, who is being smothered in his relationship with a married woman. He is an aspiring writer who has been reduced to the status of being "kept." For him to care for someone as an equal is a step forward.

Early on in this adaptation of Truman Capote's story, Paul is asked by O.J. if he thinks Holly's a phoney. Paul doesn't think so, but her friend describes Holly's strange attraction to a T: "You're wrong, she is, but on the other hand you're right, because she's a *real* phoney. You know why? Because she honestly believes all this phoney junk she believes in."

At the end, these two misfits have learned from each other and grown together. He's broken off his affair and wants to be with Holly. She, however, still fears any sort of commitment because it would mean that she has to decide what she wants to be, and that she refuses to do.

She boots her unnamed cat out of a taxi, feeling strangled by even that tenuous relationship, and then chases Paul off because she's afraid of "being caged." After nearly two hours of laughs (courtesy of George Axelrod's script and Blake Edwards' direction), the ending is the height of romantic movie drama.

As Henry Mancini's Oscar-winning score (which includes "Moon River") swells on the soundtrack, Holly wanders around in the pouring rain, desperately seeking her nameless cat. Wet and alone, she is finally forced to admit that she does need others. The three of them—man, woman, and cat—are reunited at the end.

Perhaps the reason we still care about Holly after all these years is that we can still see a little bit of her in all of us.

*DIRECTOR: Blake Edwards WITH: Audrey Hepburn, George Peppard, Patricia Neal, Martin Balsam, Buddy Ebsen, Mickey Rooney, John McGiver*

# Love Story (1970)

*L*ove Story was a ring-tailed phenomenon. When it opened at Christmas, 1970 it was the culmination of an unprecedented—and shameless—marketing campaign on the part of Paramount Pictures, author Erich Segal, publisher Avon Books and a love-starved public. The result was box office history.

The simple story concerns two young people from differing backgrounds—he (Ryan O'Neal) a well-heeled preppie and she (Ali MacGraw) a doe-eyed Italian girl—who fall in love. Then she dies. It was first an original screenplay by Erich Segal, a Yale classics professor known primarily for his popular lectures on Plautus and a tireless knack for self-promotion. Pitched to Paramount by producer Howard Minsky, the property was bought by studio head Robert Evans as a vehicle for his inamorata, MacGraw. At $2 million it was cheap—an especially attractive prospect since the studio already had $100 million tied up in stinkers like *Darling Lili, Paint Your Wagon* and *On a Clear Day You Can See Forever*. So nobody watched *Love Story* too closely.

Nobody, that is, except Minsky and Evans. They immediately had Segal "novelize" and publish his script. Paramount personnel were then ordered to purchase copies of the book at specified bookstores on certain days so as to manipulate it onto *The New York Times'* best-seller list. It worked (so much so that the *Times* subsequently stopped leaking which stores it samples) and the momentum built it into a best seller. By the time of the premiere it was a publicist's dream.

Everybody made fun of *Love Story* ("I read it while timing a three-minute egg," etc.) but nobody laughed at the $100 million it grossed to become the first modern blockbuster and save Paramount from extinction.

No one saw *Love Story* alone; mostly, women dragged men. Audiences whistled and hummed Francis Lai's mantra-like theme song, exchanged the catch phrase "Love means never having to say you're sorry" and called each other "preppie" the way Jenny (MacGraw) chided Ollie (O'Neal). By Valentine's Day, 1971, *Love Story* had received seven Oscar nominations (only Lai's music won).

To some, *Love Story* is an embarrassing relic. Its effectiveness is dulled by the histrionic acting of its two leads (unlike such classics as *Camille* or *A Star is Born*, *Love Story*'s actors seem aware they're pressing the audience's buttons). Despite this, it has become a touchstone in screen romance, and there are solid reasons why. First, its utter lack of suspense. *Love Story* is told in flashback starting with "What can you say about a 25-year-old girl who died?" There is no mystery involved, and so no tension. Like a favorite bedtime story, audiences knew what was going to happen and could abandon themselves to a relentlessly obvious process of mourning, with every new step cued by music or soap opera plotting.

Second, like *The Exorcist, Jaws* or other theatrical crowd-pleasers, once people bought their tickets a kind of roller coaster effect clicked in; audiences energized one another in line and actually swapped dares to remain dry-eyed throughout the show. Watching *Love Story* without crying became a test of cool.

Third, for those who really did want to douse their hankies. *Love Story* offered *acceptability*. Everybody was doing it. It provided a well-spaced array of "moments" to do so: the nontraditional exchange of marriage vows between Jenny and Ollie; the falling out between Ollie and his WASP father (Ray Milland); Jenny's last cup of cocoa before going to the hospital; Ollie climbing into bed with his dying wife who, only moments away from death, still looked fine.

*Love Story* is pure Hollywood hokum, but unlike much of what is made today, it is good, non-cynical hokum. It also dares to have an unhappy ending and, above all, innocence. Coming at the height of the Vietnam war, perhaps it offered young American audiences a safe opportunity to deal with love and death—a way of saying they were sorry, too.

*DIRECTOR: Arthur Hiller WITH: Ryan O'Neal, Ali MacGraw, Ray Milland, John Marley*

# An Officer and a Gentleman (1982)

Alove story can sometimes be created with only one memorable scene. For *An Officer and a Gentleman* it was that fairy-tale moment when Zack Mayo (Richard Gere) shows up in his dress whites at the paper factory where Paula Pokrifki (Debra Winger) works and literally sweeps her off her feet as we hear "Up Where We Belong," the Oscar winner for Best Song of 1982. That finale made this one of the surprise hits of the year and one of the biggest romances of the eighties.

In the course of the film, by director Taylor Hackford, Zack learns to care for others and take some responsibility for himself. "We've got a responsibility to people in our lives," says Sid Worley (David Keith) to Zack. "It's the only thing that separates us from the goddamned animals." Some nudity and rough language in Douglas Day Stewart's script are really all that separates *An Officer and a Gentleman* from countless coming-of-age romances.

When we first meet Zack he's been largely on his own. His mother is dead and his father (Robert Loggia) tells him he has "no time for this daddy stuff." Looking for direction in his life, he enrolls in naval officers's school, hoping to become a navy pilot. Sergeant Emil Foley (Louis Gossett, Jr. who won an Oscar for his performance) is the drill instructor, berating the raw recruits at every turn in hopes of making them demand the best of themselves.

Foley warns them about the "Puget Sound debs," the working-class women who have "just one thing in mind—to marry themselves a naval aviator." Zack and his buddy Sid meet some of these local women, and their parallel stories provide a dramatic counterpoint. Paula and Zack seem to be going into their romance with their eyes open. They agree that this is just a short-term thing: during his thirteen weeks of training they'll have some fun, then say goodbye.

Sid feels much the same way; he even has a fiancée back home. Linette Pomeroy (Lisa Blount) has different ideas, trying to get pregnant so that Sid will have to marry her. She loses interest when Sid declares both his love for her *and* his resignation from the navy, and their relationship ends tragically.

Meanwhile Paula and Zack find themselves falling deeper in love. Paula opens her heart, revealing that her mother had had a similar relationship with her father when *he* was in the officers' school but he then refused to marry her. Zack is so fearful of commitment, having been effectively abandoned by both his parents, that he tells her, "I don't want you to love me. I just want out."

The happy ending would ring false if we hadn't see Zack at his most vulnerable earlier in the story. At one point Sergeant Foley grants leave to everyone in the class *except* Zack and runs him through a series of brutal exercises trying to force him to quit. Zack's refusals become increasingly adamant until finally he confesses, "I have nowhere else to go."

Ultimately this is Zack's story, and not Zack and Paula's story. His reaching out to her is the climax for which we've been waiting, and it is just assumed that her life as a factory worker with no future is so dreary that of course she'll ride off with Prince Charming. Unlike the more classical construction in Gere's other Prince Charming film, *Pretty Woman* (1990), there is no need for her to change in any way except to admit that she loves him.

In *An Officer and a Gentleman*, that seems to be enough.

*DIRECTOR: Taylor Hackford WITH: Richard Gere, Debra Winger, Louis Gossett, Jr., David Keith, Lisa Blount, Robert Loggia*

# Moonstruck (1987)

From the opening credits, as Dean Martin croons "That's Amore" ("When the moon hits your eye/Like a big pizza pie/That's amore"), to the closing moments at the Brooklyn home of the Castorini family, *Moonstruck* is a sheer delight. Indeed, it is arguably the most successful romantic comedy of the eighties.

Loretta Castorini (Cher, who won the Best Actress Oscar) is a thirty-seven-year-old widow who is about to settle into a marriage of convenience with Johnny Cammareri (Danny Aiello). Johnny is a bit of a mamma's boy. His first act after their engagement is to rush off to Sicily (without Loretta) to be with his mother, supposedly on her last legs.

Johnny's parting instructions are for Loretta to go see his brother Ronny (Nicolas Cage), with whom he has not spoken in several years. Her job is simply to invite him to the wedding. What follows is not only an inconvenient romance with her fiancé's brother but a celebration of love in all its forms, both silly and serious.

Loretta's father, Cosmo (Vincent Gardenia), is trying to stave off old age by having an affair. "I can't sleep anymore," he says. "It's too much like death." His wife, Rose (Olympia Dukakis, in a role that conferred both stardom and an Oscar), knows about Cosmo's philandering, and is struggling to figure out why he does it. "Why do men chase women?" she asks, the reverse of Jean-Pierre Leaud's query "Are women magical creatures?," from François Truffaut's *Day for Night*.

All the goings-on are tied together by the full moon, when people who are "moonstruck" shed their inhibitions and confront parts of themselves and others that they usually pretend to ignore. As the characters attempt to regain control of their lives, life gets more and more confusing. Will Loretta marry the wrong brother? Will Cosmo's foolishness destroy his marriage to Rose? It is not until the final moments in the kitchen of the Castorini household that everything happily comes together.

One of the strengths of the film is that director Norman Jewison and writer John Patrick Shanley (another Oscar winner) seem honestly to like their characters. Even the most eccentric of them is given a certain amount of dignity, and so we treat them with respect rather than as cardboard cutouts mouthing wisecracks.

Although Cher's character blossoms along with her romance with Ronny, we like her from the start. She's no ugly duckling who needs to be drawn out. Her problem is that she's become too comfortable with her life and too willing to settle down with Johnny simply because he's a nice guy who won't make many demands.

Nicolas Cage's performances are an acquired taste, but here he's just right. Part of it is that his larger-than-life-size portrayal of Ronny fits perfectly with the operatic style of all the other characters. When all lovers are wearing their hearts on their sleeves, what's one more overemotional lost soul? The comparison to opera is appropriate, since it is a performance of *La Bohème* that serves as the turning point of the story.

The real standout here is Olympia Dukakis. Her Rose is a long-suffering woman who doesn't think of herself as such. She feels she's made her life and it's a pretty good one. What's she's trying to figure out is why her husband can't feel the same way. But she realizes that his running around is less a betrayal of her than a flaw within himself, and that is why she can forgive him.

It is from her wisdom that Loretta draws the strength to take charge finally of her life and her love, instead of settling down with the wrong guy and remaining nothing more than a passive bystander.

If Loretta and Ronny are "Moonstruck," don't we wish that we could be?

*DIRECTOR: Norman Jewison WITH: Cher, Nicolas Cage, Olympia Dukakis, Vincent Gardenia, Danny Aiello, John Mahoney*

71

# Crossing Delancey (1988)

One of the most notable trends of the eighties was that a large part of the Baby Boom generation was waiting longer before getting married and starting a family. Out of that trend came several films that examined women who were at a crossroads in their personal lives. *Crossing Delancey* gave us a woman who not only had an unlikely romantic choice but also had an unusual adviser on affairs of the heart: her grandmother.

Isabelle Grossman (Amy Irving) is a thirty-three-year-old woman who works in a bookstore and lives alone in New York. As far as she can tell, she is happy. Yet her "Bubbie"—still living in a Jewish enclave on the Lower East Side—cannot believe that she's happy. "She lives alone in a room, like a dog," says Bubbie (Yiddish stage star Reizl Bozyk).

Yet Isabelle and her grandmother have a special friendship that allows them to be honest with each other, as parents and children sometimes cannot be. That removed generation between them seems to open up the line of communication, and what Bubbie wants to know is why her granddaughter isn't married.

Taking matters into her own hands, Bubbie introduces Isabelle to her friend Hannah (Sylvia Miles), a marriage broker. Hannah, in turn, arranges a meeting between Isabelle and Sam (Peter Riegert), a quiet, intelligent man who has inherited his father's pickle store. Sam is nice, but this isn't the way a modern woman meets a man. Isabelle brushes him off, since she's more attracted to a local author (Jeroen Krabbe), who seems more intellectually with it. Somehow, though, Sam manages to get under her skin, and *Crossing Delancey* becomes the story of how Isabelle reconciles her continuing attraction to him.

Directed by Joan Micklin Silver, whose work includes *Hester Street* and *Chilly Scenes of Winter*, *Crossing Delancey* reminds one of the old rye bread ads that insisted "you don't have to be Jewish" to enjoy it. Just as you didn't have to be Italian to love *Moonstruck*, the warm family feeling of this film both celebrates and transcends its Jewish background.

Both Amy Irving and Peter Riegert are charming in the lead roles, playing characters more bemused than embarrassed by the situations they find themselves in. The real scene stealer, though, is Bozyk as Isabelle's Bubbie, who doesn't let her advancing years or the changing times convince her that she doesn't know that what's right is right.

"No matter how much money you have," she tells her granddaughter, "if you're alone, you're sick." Bubbie is more than just someone instigating and commenting on the romance (or lack thereof) of the main characters. She has her own life to lead, including a wonderful scene where she and other senior women practice self-defense at a neighborhood workshop. Whereas Isabelle's parents have retired at an early age to Florida, Bubbie is still fighting the good fight of being involved in life from day to day. No retirement/old age home for her.

In that sense, she serves as the perfect role model for Isabelle, who needs to know she can retain her independence even as she becomes intrigued with the traditional but easygoing Sam. Modern romance is a delicate balancing act between sometimes conflicting needs. *Crossing Delancey* tells audiences that one *can* choose wisely.

*DIRECTOR: Joan Micklin Silver WITH: Amy Irving, Peter Riegert, Reizl Bozyk, Jeroen Krabbe, Sylvia Miles*

# Pretty Woman (1990)

Millions of moviegoers saw *Pretty Woman*—many of them more than once—because they perceived it as an updated Cinderella story, a kind of modern fairy tale.

For a modern fairy tale, the cyncism behind *Pretty Woman* is staggering. It is, after all, the unlikely romance between a ruthless Wall Street raider (Richard Gere) and a "working girl" (Julia Roberts) who allows men to do anything—except kiss her. Gere's character even calls attention to their immoral kinship: "You and I are such similar creatures—we both screw people for money."

And money fuels every element of this "boy rents girl" story, for it is only by quantifying something with a dollar value that Gere's emotionally starved mogul can begin to appreciate it. Money is as meaningless to him as sex is to her, whether he's buying a corporation in order to sell off its pieces or she's just selling a piece. In a sense, the wealthy Gere and the beautiful Roberts are both saying, "If you've got it, flaunt it." The fact that most of the story is set in Beverly Hills just gilds the symbolic lily.

Crass as that sounds, it's also an explanation for the film's astounding success. The 1980s were, if nothing else, the decade in which greed was deemed to be good, and movie audiences found comfort not just in *Pretty Woman*'s skillfully contrived romance but also in the "no strings attached" rules under which its contrivance is begun. It is certainly consistent with the times: "no strings attached" was the motto of the just-concluded "me decade," what with prenuptial contracts, no-fault divorce and a junk bond economy. Likewise, Gere is first drawn to Roberts only for the convenience of sex *sans* involvement, but he eventually comes around when he realizes that unlike everyone else he hires, she doesn't need him. How much more cynical can it be than to have love grow out of rejection?

*Pretty Woman* has been compared with both *Cinderella* and *Pygmalion*, but that's not entirely accurate. It resembles *Cinderella* only in its shameless wish fulfillment, and *Pygmalion* because it appears to be about a man who falls in love with his own creation. In fact, Gere does *not* create Roberts—he barely pays attention during the film's celebrated couturier sequence and is absent from its single etiquette lesson. There is no apparent reason why Roberts' character should grow from vulgarian into sophisticate. She just does, but by the time Gere becomes thoroughly taken with her, the viewer has also shed all resistance to the idea. There are reasons for this: In movie logic, she becomes worthy of Gere by crying at an opera, refusing (at one point) to take his money and—breaking her own professional rule—kissing the client.

*Pretty Woman* finally succeeds at being romantic because it is about characters who deny their romance. Naturally, the audience expects all along they'll fall in love, which is why the script's original ending—in which Gere and Roberts break up and never see each other again—was quickly changed. The Disney/Touchstone studio and director Garry Marshall were not stupid. Like Preston Sturges before them, they realized that their most enthusiastic cheerleaders were the audience, and they eagerly encouraged this conspiracy with a happy plot resolution and a splendid menagerie of character actors, notably Hector Elizondo as an obsequious hotel manager.

*Pretty Woman* is a throwback to the studio films of the thirties and forties, when women bought tickets to see what Ginger Rogers was wearing and men went along to see how Clark Gable would control any situation. In 1990 audiences wanted love, even love that was mutually exploitative.

*DIRECTOR: Garry Marshall WITH: Richard Gere, Julia Roberts, Hector Elizondo*

# Hello, Young Lovers

*Youth may be wasted on the young, but certain love stories can help the younger generation gain experience. Remember that first crush? Those naughty (yet naïve) thoughts? The pain of saying the right thing at the wrong time? So does Hollywood.*

# The Clock (1945)

The title object of this Vincente Minnelli drama has both an actual and symbolic meaning. Literally it is the clock at the Astor Hotel, under which Manhattan secretary Alice Mayberry (Judy Garland) and Corporal Joe Allen (Robert Walker) agree to meet for a date. Figuratively it represents the pressure of time: Allen is due to report back on duty in two days.

Within forty-eight hours they will meet, fall in love, get married, and part. Unlike the lovers in the pressure-cooker atmosphere of Indonesia in *The Year of Living Dangerously*, we know these two are going to be reunited after the war, settling down to the comforts of home and hearth.

Audiences who only know Walker as the pathological Bruno Anthony in Alfred Hitchcock's *Strangers on a Train* (1951) may not realize that he was cast against type in that film. Throughout the forties he appeared as a series of wide-eyed innocents, often going off to war in movies like *See Here, Private Hargrove* and *Since You Went Away* (both 1944). *The Clock* offers him the best of those roles; he wanders around Grand Central Station wondering what to do with his free time in a strange city, looking like a lovable stray puppy ("I'm green as grass," he admits).

His meeting with Alice is the stuff of screwball comedy; he rushes to her aid when her heel gets caught in an escalator. As Alice, Garland brings a nice sense of underplaying in her first dramatic role. She's no floozy looking to be picked up, just someone who can't help but respond to this young innocent alone in the big city.

Their first date is all hearts and flowers, as they talk and talk, discovering how much they enjoy each other. After an evening walk in the park (it's 1945, remember), they hitch a ride with a milkman (James Gleason) out on his deliveries. When the milkman is dealt a blow by a boisterous drunk (Keenan Wynn), the young couple complete his deliveries for him.

The comedy turns to drama when they are separated in a crowded subway station and realize they have no way to find each other. They both return to where they met and, upon discovering her, Joe's first remark is "Quick! What's your name?"

Now they are literally racing against the clock as they decide to marry before Joe must leave for duty. "We'll never be more sure," he argues. "We might never have found one another again." They face delay after delay: blood tests, waiting periods which must be waived by a judge, and a justice of the peace rushing to make his commuter train. When they're finally married it's almost anticlimactic. "It was so ugly," sobs Alice.

In a touching scene they wander into a church and, sitting in the quiet sanctuary, read aloud the wedding service, giving themselves the dignity and ceremony they were earlier denied. This is a love so pure and true you just know these kids are going to make it.

The final scene shows Joe and Alice parting at the train station, with other wives seeing other husbands off to the war. As Alice departs, Minnelli's camera pulls up and away so that Alice blends into the swirling crowd around her. There are love stories all around us, he is saying, if only we knew to stop and look.

In one sense Minnelli was right about the possibility of romance being right under one's nose. After he finished filming *The Clock*, he married Garland.

*DIRECTOR: Vincente Minnelli WITH: Judy Garland, Robert Walker, James Gleason, Keenan Wynn*

# David and Lisa (1963)

No setting could be less conducive to romance than that of *David and Lisa*. David Clemmons (Keir Dullea) is a deeply troubled youth who escapes his possessive parents' expectations by denying all emotion and becoming hysterical at the slightest touch. Lisa Brandt (Janet Margolin) is a schizophrenic girl who speaks in rhyme so as to impose order upon an imposing world. Both have been sent to a suburban sanitarium/school for "exceptional" teens. Neither takes comfort in the ironic label.

The story of *David and Lisa*—which Frank Perry directed with caring restraint from his wife Eleanor's intricately simplified script—is how each finds a path back to sanity by first finding the other. Based on the clinical study *Lisa and David* by Theodore Isaac Rubin, this small, independently produced film captured hearts and numerous awards with its nonsensationalized portrayal of mental illness. Unlike *Ordinary People* (1980), which covered similar territory, *David and Lisa* demonstrated that therapy is a *process* rather than a convenient plot device, and in showing the delicate stages its characters pass through it becomes genuinely, quietly and profoundly moving.

But David Clemmons and Lisa Brandt don't fall in love; they fall in trust. Initially resisting their respective therapists at the sanitorium (hers is Clifton James, his is Howard Da Silva in his first screen role since the McCarthy-era blacklist), they discover that they share a mutual understanding of loneliness. In effect, they must cure themselves—the burned leading the burned.

Their relationship, like their sanity, is built on incident: David sees that Lisa is threatened by authority figures, so he develops compassion; Lisa promises never to touch David, so he begins to trust; David deduces that Lisa responds to rhyme, so he practices communicating.

*David and Lisa* is about loneliness. All of the students at the sanitorium are shunned by society, but as loners within the peer group David and Lisa are outcasts among outcasts. The hell they all share, of course, is that all of them know that they are, as one of the neighbors so tactfully yells, "a bunch of screwballs spoiling this town."

Responds David, "If you're normal, who wants to be normal?" But in point of fact they all desperately do, with each face registering the pain inside. What viewer can fail to be moved by their desire to belong? When at the end Lisa abandons her rhyming and David permits her to touch his hand, it is a tiny victory for mankind but an earth-shaking moment for David and Lisa. This is where the real love story starts.

It is also the point at which the film comes to symbolize all the anguish of adolescence. David Clemmons and Lisa Brandt are no longer merely a mentally disturbed boy and girl; they are, in a universal sense, all young people who have ever felt isolated from parents, peers and a world that seems poised to devour. As every awkward teenager discovers, the only people worthy of trust are other teenagers. It is only later, when they become adults, that they come to understand this reaching-out process.

*DIRECTOR: Frank Perry WITH: Keir Dullea, Janet Margolin, Howard Da Silva*

# Bikini Beach (1964)

When the front end of the Baby Boom generation began hitting adolescence in the late fifties and early sixties, Hollywood understood they represented a huge potential audience. Those young couples wanted some place to go to on a date, and no one realized this better than James H. Nicholson and Samuel Z. Arkoff of American International Pictures, who churned out picture after picture intended for the teen crowd.

In 1963 the two producers found the mother lode with a movie called *Beach Party*. Over the next three years it was followed by *Muscle Beach Party*, *Bikini Beach* and *Pajama Party* (all 1964), *Beach Blanket Bingo* and *How to Stuff a Wild Bikini* (both 1965), and *Ghost in the Invisible Bikini* (1966). While the cast and storylines were constantly changing, the movies were always about teenagers in love.

The young stars would sing, dance, surf and otherwise celebrate being teenagers. The bad guys were all clowns, whether it was Eric von Zipper (Harvey Lembeck doing Marlon Brando in *The Wild One*) or some Hollywood veteran guest starring as the killjoy adult trying to ruin their fun. For teens out on a date, it was lightweight entertainment that reinforced their view of the world without requiring them to pay too much attention to it.

In *Bikini Beach* the killjoy is Keenan Wynn as Harvey Huntington Honeywagon III ("honeywagon" is slang for the portable toilets brought on location shoots), who wants to chase the surfing guys and gals away from retirement homes he is developing near the beach. He claims that teens are only interested in the three S's: "surfing, speed and sex" (the "speed" in this case refers not to drugs but to hot rods).

What's interesting is to see what passes for teenage lasciviousness in the early sixties. Honeywagon claims that the teenagers have "an abnormal preoccupation with sex." Yet when Frankie (Frankie Avalon) says to Dee Dee (Annette Funicello) that her girlfriends are "children" and urges her to come down to the beach for some moonlit romance, she replies, "You go listen to the moon and the waves. Until I hear wedding bells, I'm children, too."

Teen idol Frankie Avalon and ex-Mouseketeer Annette Funicello were hardly a danger to the morals of America. Their romance in *Bikini Beach* is threatened by the arrival of British pop idol "The Potato Bug" (also played by Avalon). For those who don't get the reference, Frankie criticizes the girls for having "gone *beetle* over a potato bug." In the end, though, they realize they really do love each other, and the teens win their battle with Honeywagon as well. There's even time for "Little" Stevie Wonder to do a song.

Two decades later, Frankie and Annette were reunited for *Back to the Beach* (1987), which has them cast as parents trying to understand *their* kids. Frankie has become a Ford dealer in Ohio while Annette now has to deal with a daughter living with her boyfriend. Unfortunately, the movie wasn't pitched to grown-up Boomers looking for a little silly nostalgia but to contemporary teens. After John Hughes' movies like *Sixteen Candles* (1984) and *The Breakfast Club* (1985), the world of the beach party film might as well have been *Love Finds Andy Hardy* (1938) for all the connection it had to modern teen life.

Movies likes *Bikini Beach* were a product of a long-gone era. Within a few years, when the Frankies and Annettes in the audience were facing the realities of civil rights, Vietnam and psychedelic experimentation, the antics of the *Beach Party* crew became irrelevant. For a short time, though, they represented Hollywood's comic vision of teenage love.

*DIRECTOR: William Asher WITH: Frankie Avalon, Annette Funicello, Keenan Wynn, Harvey Lembeck, Don Rickles, Martha Hyer, Stevie Wonder*

# West Side Story (1961)

# Romeo and Juliet (1968)

Star-crossed lovers have always been a good subject for romance, but *young* star-crossed lovers such as Romeo and Juliet (and their modern counterparts, Tony and Maria) are special. This is partly because Fate seems most cruel when it leans on people whose lives are before them. Or more cynically, it is the elevation of self-centered teenage anguish to the level of great tragedy that has assured these stories' appeal.

*Romeo and Juliet* had been filmed at least five times before Italian director Franco Zeffirelli decided to do it with two stars whose ages (seventeen and sixteen) roughly matched those of Shakespeare's characters (seventeen and fifteen). What Leonard Whiting and Olivia Hussey lacked in training they made up for with energy, and in 1968 the motion picture became the dating movie of the season (although an equal number of younger kids first saw it on school field trips).

Gorgeously photographed (by Oscar-winning Pasquale De Santis) and notorious for its split-second glimpse of Romeo's rump, the self-proclaimed "now" production made the lovers seem more like rebels against an oppressive government Establishment, a fitting (if not entirely accurate) lure for a young moviegoing generation sweating the equally divisive Vietnam War. If Shakespeare could be called "countercultural," *Romeo and Juliet* was it—a naughty but *bona fide* classic for an alienated generation.

So, in its day, was *West Side Story*, the Arthur Laurents/Leonard Bernstein/Stephen Sondheim transposition of *Romeo and Juliet* into the milieu of New York's Hell's Kitchen street gangs. In today's atmosphere of brutal crack murders, the switchblade-flicking tough guys of the American "Jets" and the Puerto Rican "Sharks" seem tame, especially when they slip into Jerome Robbins' lithe dance steps. But in 1961 the film broke cinematic ground (as it had on the stage in the fifties) with its realistic portrayal of the torment of modern youth.

As with its source material, *West Side Story* features the American Tony (Richard Beymer) and the Puerto Rican Maria (Natalie Wood), whose brief liaison challenges their separate "family" loyalties. But unlike Shakespeare's play, in which a dejected Romeo and Juliet take their own lives, Maria refuses to follow a murdered Tony to the grave, choosing instead to fight for tolerance between the warring gangs. In a society where teen suicides have become a national epidemic, no change could be more hopeful, even if the film's dated slang and glossy patina have made it a little klunky.

*Romeo and Juliet* and *West Side Story* share similar magic moments, and one of the joys is comparing how the latter film updates the former. The balcony on which the lovers tryst becomes its modern urban equivalent, a fire escape; the Capulet ball at which they first meet becomes a dance at the local gym; the admonishing Prince is turned into the omnipresent Officer Krupke; and so forth. The music in both films is haunting (although the song dubbing for Beymer, Wood and Moreno makes for a strange soundtrack album in which none of the leads does his own singing), and Nino Rota's score for *Romeo and Juliet* even made the 1968 pop charts!

Over the years others have reinterpreted Shakespeare: *Othello* became *A Double Life*, *Taming of the Shrew* became *Kiss Me, Kate*, *Macbeth* became *Men of Respect* and *Throne of Blood*, and *The Tempest* became *Forbidden Planet*. But the most successful transpositions are those involving romance, and both *Romeo and Juliet* and *West Side Story* have romance to die for.

*West Side Story: DIRECTORS: Robert Wise and Jerome Robbins WITH: Natalie Wood, Richard Beymer, Rita Moreno, George Chakiris, Russ Tamblyn*

*Romeo and Juliet: DIRECTOR: Franco Zeffirelli WITH: Leonard Whiting, Olivia Hussey, Milo O'Shea, Michael York*

# Urban Cowboy (1980)

Screen romance—and, for that matter, real-life romance—dwells on the joys of young love and avoids the harsh reality that often accompanies it. The conflict comes when young men and women try to live their lives "just like in the movies" only to discover that it's harder than Hollywood makes it look.

The 1970s had not been a romantic era in Hollywood. Except for an occasional *The Goodbye Girl* or the first *Rocky*, Hollywood forsook relationships in favor of car chases, space ships and sharks. People were still falling in love, but the movies had apparently given up on telling them how.

*Urban Cowboy* is a film that was aware of this contradiction. Furthermore, it paired the electric John Travolta with the sultry new Debra Winger in a highly charged love affair that was also one of the first Hollywood movies to address the growing tensions between men and women in the wake of the Women's Movement.

It signaled a monumental change for Travolta, whose streetwise persona in *Saturday Night Fever* in 1977 and *Grease* in 1978 made him the screen's first new male sex symbol in years. But his first films appealed primarily to teens; could he somehow broaden his image? The solution came from writer-director James Bridges who, with journalist Aaron Latham, adapted Latham's *Esquire* magazine profile of a Houston, Texas honkytonk/dating bar called Gilley's.

Travolta stars as Bud Davis, freshly arrived from Spur, Texas to work in Houston's busy oil refineries. He labors by day but lives for the nights when he can hang out at Gilley's where he joins other citified men to don Stetsons, drink beer and roam the concrete prairie. Like everyone who walks into Gilley's (and the thousands of other pickup spots then opening across America), he is looking for love.

As it happened, "Lookin' for Love"—a song from the film's country-western soundtrack—became the anthem for a generation of dating singles. No single phrase better captured the quest of the Me Generation, and the electricity that sparked between the film's two romantic leads.

"You a real cowboy?" the spunky Sissy (Winger) asks Bud one night at the bar.

"Well," Bud drawls, "that depends on what you think a real cowboy is." They then begin a dance together that quickly becomes a fertility ritual. It doesn't take a genius to break the code: *Urban Cowboy* is all about masculinity. It appears constantly, if casually: Travolta proves his manhood by picking up two bimbos on his first night at Gilley's; he endures grueling work hours to build a nest-egg for eventual marriage; he gets drunk; he picks fights. But when he orders Sissy around and then slaps her when she talks back, we know he is following the wrong map.

"You're not supposed to hit girls!" she fumes, and it's clear that he had assumed it was his birthright. But they make good love together, so they marry and move into a house trailer where their lives quickly settle into a fast-food existence—marriage, after all, involves more than sex. Nevertheless, when Bud persists in treating Sissy like his servant, she leaves him for Wes (Scott Glenn), an ex-convict whom she deems "a real cowboy." She only returns to Bud when Wes's brand of "real cowboy" turns out to be a man who beats women not because it's what he knows, but because it's what he likes.

The real test of manhood, of control, is Gilley's celebrated mechanical bull. When—under Wes's tutelage—Sissy performs better than her husband on the phallic surrogate, it cuckolds Bud and sets the stage for a bitter three-way showdown. When it is finally resolved, Bud and Sissy have a clearer idea of the role each is to play in the future. For starters, they realize that they are now two adults who owe each other certain responsibilities.

*Urban Cowboy* was a telling chronicle of the pressures that young lovers faced in a new, grown-up era.

*DIRECTOR—CO-WRITER: James Bridges WITH: John Travolta, Debra Winger, Scott Glenn*

# Sixteen Candles (1984)

With *Sixteen Candles*, writer-director John Hughes laid claim to the teenage film. Other filmmakers would try, but films that Hughes made himself or farmed out to others would be the ones that struck home with teenage audiences in the eighties: *The Breakfast Club, Pretty in Pink, Some Kind of Wonderful.*

The storyline is simply two days in the life of Samantha Baker (Molly Ringwald). Day one is her sixteenth birthday, which her entire family seems to have forgotten because her older sister Ginny (Blanche Baker) is getting married. Day two is the wedding day.

In the course of these two days, Hughes depicts a good deal of the fun, the foibles and the fantasies of modern adolescent life, ending with Samantha and her dream date Jake (Michael Schoeffling) having a quiet moment together.

"Happy birthday, Samantha. Make a wish," says Jake.

"It's already come true," she replies.

Hughes shows us the basic insecurities of teenagers, and his ability to do so is the reason teens find that Hughes's films ring true. Anthony Michael Hall plays Ted, a character universally referred to (even in the film's credits) as "the Geek." Naturally he doesn't see himself that way. He imagines himself a swinging dude. When he and Samantha are exchanging secrets, his darkest confession is "I never bagged a babe." This hardly makes him alone among high school freshmen, but Hughes understands that *every* teenage boy thinks he is the only one in the world with that particular "flaw".

Sam is similarly insecure. Examining herself in the mirror, she tells herself, "You need four inches of bod and a great birthday." In school, she takes a "confidential quiz" about her sex life. "Have you ever done it?" the quiz asks. "I don't think so," she writes.

When she reveals to a friend that she has a crush on Jake, her friend tells her, "He doesn't even know you exist." Adolescence is a time when all emotions are larger than life and rejection can seem like the end of the world. It is, indeed, a very cruel age.

Hughes adopts that adolescent cruelty as well, which is why the film was such a teen hit. The Chinese exchange student (Gedde Watanabe) living with Sam's grandparents sports a name that's a dirty joke, Long Duk Dong. A young Joan Cusack appears in several scenes in a neck brace, and is identified as "Geek Girl #1" in the credits. And dream date Jake palms off his semi-conscious girlfriend Caroline (Haviland Morris) on Ted the Geek, assuring him that she's so drunk she won't know the difference.

As in most of Hughes's films, he takes the side of adolescents versus the adults but allows for at least one adult who is sensitive to the feelings of his young heroes. Here it is Sam's father (Paul Dooley), who apologizes to her for forgetting her birthday and promises her that when she meets the right guy "it'll be forever."

*Sixteen Candles* made Molly Ringwald a teen star, and she's been trying to grow beyond that ever since. In the meantime, Hughes continues his fascination with the life of kids and teenagers (*Uncle Buck, Home Alone*) and adults who act like kids and teenagers (*She's Having a Baby, Planes, Trains and Automobiles*).

Yet for all its wild parties and slapstick humor, the moment everyone remembers from *Sixteen Candles* is a sixteen-year-old girl and an eighteen-year-old boy, sharing some birthday cake and a chaste kiss.

*DIRECTOR: John Hughes WITH: Molly Ringwald. Michael Schoeffling, Anthony Michael Hall, Paul Dooley, Blanche Baker, Haviland Morris, John Cusack, Joan Cusack, Gedde Watanabe*

# Dirty Dancing (1987)

"That was the summer of 1963, when everybody called me 'Baby' and it didn't occur to me to mind," says Baby Houseman (Jennifer Grey) at the start of this surprise hit from the summer of 1987. This coming-of-age story took audiences by surprise and became one of the sleeper hits of the year, elevating Patrick Swayze to heartthrob status.

Our focus is eighteen-year-old Baby, as she learns about love and heartache and duplicity, and all the other fun things one experiences upon becoming an adult. She and her family are spending a few weeks at Kellerman's, a family resort in the Catskills (actually shot in Virginia) operated by Max Kellerman (Jack Weston). While Dr. Jake Houseman (Jerry Orbach) just wants to relax, his daughter Baby quickly attracts the attention of several of the young men at the hotel. Max's grandson informs her that he's "the catch of the county," but she only has eyes for Johnny Castle (Swayze), the muscular dance instructor.

Baby, who is as innocent as her name suggests, thinks that Johnny is in love with Penny (Cynthia Rhodes), his glamorous co-instructor. In fact they are just friends, as Baby realizes after she is forced to come to their assistance when another member of the staff gets Penny pregnant.

Grey, daughter of *Cabaret* star Joel Grey, got her first starring role here and managed to capture that moment when one teeters between childhood and growing up. Her scenes with Orbach, where they must both come to terms with the fact that she really is no longer a baby, are especially powerful for not patronizing either character.

It is her relationship with Johnny that is the real point of the film, however, after she has to take Penny's place at a hotel show where they were to perform. It is their rehearsal time together that best brings back the memories of the old Astaire-Rogers films, where choreography equals seduction.

No doubt nostalgia, too, played a big part in helping *Dirty Dancing* find its audience. The pre-Beatles '60s soundtrack included "Be My Baby," "Big Girls Don't Cry" and "In the Still of the Nite." Set only months before the assassination of President Kennedy, the film is in many ways a salute to America's loss of innocence, not just Baby's.

Hollywood being Hollywood, the movie had to be made relevant for modern audiences. The opening credits hinted that it was the era's music that led to the sexually suggestive dancing we see, but the music here seems positively Victorian by comparison to current teen hits. What made *Dirty Dancing* appealing was not that it was "dirty" but that it was so innocent.

The movie builds up to a cathartic production number at the end, in which everyone is reconciled and the wild dancing of the teenagers is accepted by their elders. Earlier, when Baby went to a staff party where everyone was dancing up a storm, she was asked, "Can you imagine dancing like that on the main floor—home of the family fox trot? Max would close the place down first."

Director Emile Ardolino, who made his name with his dance films and television programs, including the Oscar-winning documentary *He Makes Me Feel Like Dancin'*, uses dance to bring out his characters' feelings. If there is a moment in the film where Baby becomes a woman, it is not when she is in bed, but when she is dancing.

Near the end of the film Max tells his bandleader (dance great Charles Honi Coles) that he feels an era is ending. While this sounds more like dialogue written in 1987 rather than actually spoken in 1963, it was certainly true for Baby and Johnny. When they met on the dance floor, their lives would never be the same again.

*DIRECTOR: Emile Ardolino WITH: Jennifer Gray, Patrick Swayze, Jerry Orbach, Cynthia Rhodes, Jack Weston*

# CHAPTER FIVE

# Breaking Up is Hard to Do

*The heart is amazingly resilient, especially where Hollywood romance is concerned. These are films in which lovers emerge sadder, wiser, and—in almost every case—alone. Despite this, audiences see through the tears to embrace them as classics.*

# Camille (1936)

The unabashedly romantic *Camille* had already been filmed no fewer than six times before Greta Garbo starred as Alexandre Dumas *fils*'s tragic "Lady of the Camellias" under George Cukor's direction in 1936. But this eternal version was produced two years after Hollywood revamped its stern Production Code to purge the screen of exactly the kind of material that *Camille* was about.

Set in the Paris of 1847, the story followed the fated liaison of young Armand Duvall (Robert Taylor) and Marguerite Gauthier (Greta Garbo), a scintillating and magnetically beautiful courtesan. Although she sells her favors to the lubricious Baron de Varville (Henry Daniell), her heart clearly (and freely) belongs to Armand. It is only when Armand's father (Lionel Barrymore) begs her to stay away from his son that Marguerite—by now dying of tuberculosis—truly proves her love by sending Armand away. When the end is near Armand returns, learns the tearful truth, and takes his beloved in his arms one last time.

At least, that was *Camille* according to the Production Code; Dumas's version was much more ironic and definitely more amorous. For one thing, in the novel Marguerite and Armand go off together to the country, as in the film, but they do more there than just pick flowers. Furthermore, this love nest is financed with money Marguerite receives from a Duke who treats her like the daughter he once loved. Finally, in the book Armand still goes abroad to forget Marguerite, but he returns too late to see her alive.

What the movie *Camille* lacked in literary faithfulness, it more than exceeded in passion. Demimondes like Marguerite drip world-weariness like jewelry, and Mlle. Gauthier did not disappoint, especially when it came to acknowledging her tarnished past:

"But Marguerite," chides her friend, Nichette (Elizabeth Allen), "it's ideal to love—and to marry the one you love."

"I have no faith in ideals," Marguerite responds.

Later she meets Armand, whom she mistakes for a rich man, and flirts with him: "I'm not always sincere—one can't be in this world, you know. But I am not sorry the mistake happened."

Finally, once she has resigned herself to death and loneliness, she tells Armand, "Perhaps it's better if I live in your heart—where the world can't see me."

Under the strict Production Code, a woman in Marguerite's position had to suffer for her sins or, preferably, die. *Camille* managed both, and it well suited the purpose of the filmmakers, who rearranged the doom-laden elements of her life until they formed a soap opera worthy of the grand sets and flowing costumes.

As for Garbo, she abandoned her customary Swedish languidness in favor of a vivacious coquetry that, despite its purpose in the story, never became vulgar. Director Cukor, as usual, can be thanked for having taste. Like Meryl Streep when she's not playing one of her dour, accented roles, Garbo actually seems to be having a good time.

Most people, however, remember the film not for its laughter but for its tears. In part, they are shed for lost innocence—like that first true love whose fond recollection secretly sustains us for a lifetime. *Camille* is a flower pressed between the pages of a diary, a keepsake that lives only in that soft-focus memory we accord a cherished movie.

*DIRECTOR: George Cukor WITH: Greta Garbo, Robert Taylor, Lionel Barrymore, Henry Daniell*

# The Philadelphia Story (1940)

On one level *The Philadelphia Story* is about how C. K. Dexter Haven (Cary Grant) wins back his socialite ex-wife Tracy Lord (Katharine Hepburn) from her social-climbing fiancé (John Howard). Yet our real interest is in the moon-drenched romance between Tracy and magazine reporter Macaulay "Mike" Connor (James Stewart) rather than her relationship with either of the other men.

In a brief opening scene we see the breakup of her first marriage. Dex stalks out of their home with his baggage. Tracy follows with his shoes and golf bag. She drops the shoes at his feet, and breaks one of the clubs over her knee. Dex follows her back, raises his arms as if to strike her, but instead just shoves her to the floor. They are both incredibly childish ("You might say we grew up together," he remarks later).

Two years pass, and Dex is now the bemused bystander who playfully helps sneak the reporter and his photographer Liz Imbrie (Ruth Hussey) into the Lord mansion to cover the society wedding of the season. The Hollywood star system being what it is, we know that Tracy must end up with Dex, since Cary Grant was already a star, whereas Stewart had only achieved fame the year before with *Mr. Smith Goes to Washington* and *Destry Rides Again*. (Stewart would go on to win an Oscar for *The Philadelphia Story*).

Yet the scenes between Stewart and Hepburn are the most charged moments in the film. They dislike each other from the start. She resents his presence, especially since the only reason she must allow it is that his magazine is threatening to expose her father's philandering. He has decided, before they've even met, that she's a "young, rich, rapacious American female—there's no other country where she exists."

In the course of their weekend together, they break down the barriers between them, barriers that turn out to be the cause of their problems with much of the rest of the world. Tracy has such imperious standards that she not only chased Dex away but has been estranged from her father as well. Mike has so armored himself with his cynicism that he's stunned when his partner/girl friend reveals in casual conversation that she'd been previously married.

On the night before the wedding the two of them find themselves alone together, full of champagne and unspoken thoughts. She calls him an "intellectual snob" because he has never seen her as a person, only a representative of her class. "The fact is you can't be a first-rate writer or a first-rate human being until you've learned to have some small regard for human frailty," she says, cutting herself off in mid-word as she realizes she is describing herself as well.

Suddenly he *does* see the real her, and he is enchanted. "You're a golden girl, Tracy," he says, "full of life and warmth and delight." Soon they are kissing ("Golly," she gasps) and thinking it is true love.

In harsh daylight, however, what they have is better than love. They have learned to be considerate of and honest with other people. They really don't belong together (indeed, it is the only film Hepburn and Stewart ever made together), but they have helped each other become better people. By film's end, everyone is with whom they should be.

Perhaps the greatest triumph of all was that of Katharine Hepburn. She had been labeled "box office poison" by theater owners in 1938 and departed Hollywood for Broadway. She starred in the stage hit *The Philadelphia Story*, which Philip Barry had written specifically for her. In a shrewd move, she had control of the screen rights to the play, so that when Hollywood came calling they were obliged to cast her as the "unapproachable" Tracy Lord . . . and soon her "box office poison" days were over for good.

*DIRECTOR: George Cukor WITH: Cary Grant, Katharine Hepburn, James Stewart, Ruth Hussey, John Howard, Henry Daniell*

# Casablanca (1942)

When Ingrid Bergman was making *Casablanca* she had a problem. Was her character, Ilsa Lund, supposed to end up with her lover, Rick (Humphrey Bogart), or return to her husband, Victor Laszlo (Paul Henreid)? In an interview years later with writer Richard Anobile, she admitted that until they shot the ending of the film, nobody knew for sure. As a result, when Ilsa appears confused over what to do ("You'll have to think for both of us," she tells Rick), she was being utterly sincere.

Much has been written about the film over the years. When the late Harry Reasoner hung up his hat as a regular correspondent on television's *60 Minutes*, it was his most requested piece—on *Casablanca*—that served as his swan song. Perhaps the best explanation for the film's endless appeal is that it stands for a love being so grand that one is willing to sacrifice it for something even greater.

Supposedly two endings were written, one with Ilsa going off with Victor and one with her remaining behind with Rick. After shooting the first ending, they realized that there was no need to film the alternative. "I'm no good at being noble," says Rick in the scene that shows him unequaled at being noble, "but it doesn't take much to see that the problems of three little people don't amount to a hill o' beans in this crazy world."

Half a century later what amazes most about *Casablanca*, considered by many to be one of Hollywood's greatest achievements, was how much of an accident it all was. Based on a flop play (*Everybody Goes to Rick's*), this was going to be just another film off the Hollywood assembly line. The Hollywood trade papers originally carried the news that Warner Bros.' new film would star Ronald Reagan, Ann Sheridan, and Dennis Morgan.

Instead, with Bogart, Bergman, Henreid, Claude Rains, Peter Lorre, Sydney Greenstreet, Conrad Veidt, and Dooley Wilson (who sings "As Time Goes By"), *Casablanca* won several Oscars, including Best Picture. The script (an Oscar winner for Julius J. and Philip G. Epstein and Howard Koch) is so polished that every line is memorable. We laugh at Rick's dry humor (claiming he came to Casablanca "for the waters," he is told that the city is in the desert; he replies, "I was misinformed"). We cheer Captain Louis Renault (Rains) when he reacts to the murder of Nazi bad guy Major Strasser (Veidt) by saying, "Round up the usual suspects."

Director Michael Curtiz (another Oscar winner) was asked for years about the success of *Casablanca* and was at a loss to explain—or duplicate—its magic. Although his distinguished film career includes *Yankee Doodle Dandy* and *Mildred Pierce*, his attempt to consciously recreate *Casablanca* with most of the same cast was the disappointing *Passage to Marseilles* (1944).

Years later Woody Allen would open *Play It Again, Sam* (1972) with the closing scene of *Casablanca*, and close with him and Diane Keaton replaying it almost verbatim. "That's beautiful," says Keaton.

"It's from *Casablanca*," replies Allen, "I waited my whole life to say it."

Perhaps Woody Allen has put his finger on it. Rick represents an ideal in the way Victor Laszlo cannot. Victor, after all, is a hero: he's fought the Nazis, he's been keeping one step ahead of the Gestapo, and he's risked his own safety for Ilsa. Rick is just an ordinary guy who claims, "I stick my neck out for nobody," but who learns that romantic sacrifice isn't only the province of heroes.

At the end Rick doesn't get the girl, but he regains his soul and has the promise of a "beautiful friendship" as he walks off to join the Free French with Louis Renault. It's a happy ending, for as Rick reminds Ilsa, "We'll always have Paris."

*DIRECTOR: Michael Curtiz WITH: Humphrey Bogart, Ingrid Bergman, Paul Henreid, Claude Rains, Conrad Veidt, Dooley Wilson, Sydney Greenstreet, Peter Lorre, S. Z. Sakall*

# Brief Encounter (1945)

They say the British are terrible lovers, but as *Brief Encounter* attests, it's not for lack of trying. Based on Noel Coward's *Still Life*, a one-act play about an unconsummated love affair between a middle-class doctor (Trevor Howard) and a housewife (Celia Johnson) who are both married to others, it was filmed by David Lean as a full-out melodrama that possesses all the dignity of its properly improper central characters. The story itself is both dated and timeless—dated in its presentation of conservative mores, yet timeless in its resilience; *Brief Encounter* is the film that Glenda Jackson and George Segal cry over in *A Touch of Class* (1972), with which it has a great deal in common—except sex.

It begins innocently enough: Waiting for a train after her regular Thursday shopping, Johnson gets some grit in her eye that is removed by passing physician Howard, whose train takes him in the opposite direction. Each week their fleeting encounters take on added meaning and last longer; they meet for lunch; they begin attending the cinema (fittingly, to see *Flames of Passion*); they kiss; they fall in love. On one occasion they plan a nervous assignation in a friend's apartment, only to be interrupted. One day he announces he is taking a job in Africa and they must part. Although she wants to commit suicide by throwing herself under a train, she instead goes home where her husband (Cyril Raymond) is waiting.

*Brief Encounter* unfolds in flashback through Johnson's monologues as she recounts the story the way she wishes she could tell her husband Fred—who may, in fact, suspect it already. This novelistic techniques allows Lean and Coward to say what their actors cannot. The single event where Howard and Johnson realize they are in love comes at the most mundane moment: he is speaking enthusiastically about preventive medicine and she is pretending to listen, when the camera slowly moves in on her and Rachmaninoff's Piano Concerto #2 ( a recurrent theme) plays in the background. Their faces begin to glow with recognition, but only slightly. The camera pulls back and their feelings are established without specific words.

"We must be sensible," Johnson insists at one point, to which Howard responds, sensibly, "It's too late to be sensible."

What stands between them is not politeness but fear. Their liaison lasts only a few weeks; it is intense, yet inhibited. Historian Roger Manvell has noted that the lovers' quandary is symbolized by the commuter trains that form a motif: the nonstop express, with whistles that punctuate their depot meetings, represents the passion they cannot give way to, while their own locals remind them of their daily humdrum lives and obligations. Significantly, when Johnson considers suicide, it is under the wheels of an express train—again, an action she cannot follow through.

The absolute propriety of *Brief Encounter* (though they have lusted in heart if not in deed) is what makes it work. In dramatic terms it is called "playing against the scene": the technique of letting the audience complete the emotion that the actor does not show. The film's skillful contrast of supercharged situations with underplayed performances is the reason *Brief Encounter* is still cited as the greatest romance to come out of England since Edward VIII gave up the throne for the woman he loved.

*DIRECTOR: David Lean WITH: Celia Johnson, Trevor Howard*

# Splendor in the Grass (1961)

If it were not so achingly perceptive, *Splendor in the Grass* would be just another teen picture about the pain of growing up. As it is, Elia Kazan's film (from William Inge's Oscar-winning original script) hits all the bases with cleats on but manages to do so with a sense of irony that makes it more sympathetic than pandering.

It is a relentless story of unrequited love: Natalie Wood and Warren Beatty (in his first film) are teenagers in starched, parched southeastern Kansas, 1928. Although they are passionately in love, they remain chaste in accordance with the conservative morality of Prohibition-era America. It isn't easy, especially with Beatty's despotic father (Pat Hingle) and Wood's ceaselessly critical mother (Joanna Roos) sending them into each other's confidence. When Beatty, unable to stifle his sexual anguish (or "goin' nuts," as he tells his unhearing doctor), gets release with the town harlot, Wood has an emotional breakdown. By the time she recovers two and a half years later he is married and she is about to wed. To free herself, she locates him on his farm, where they both say goodbye while desperately hiding the embers of love and reconciling themselves to average lives in which they "don't think much about happiness."

*Splendor in the Grass* formed Warren Beatty's screen image. As the physically gifted but emotionally stunted Bud Stamper, Beatty found the contradiction that has served him for over three decades. Bud has it all—looks, money, brains, athletic prowess and popularity. But he is also unable to overcome the plans his domineering father has laid out for him. He is trapped; he vents steam not at those who deserve it—his parents—but on the football field, in parking lot melees, or against himself by flunking out of school. Beatty saw that when a character is unhappy, it's just begging for sympathy, but when a Golden Boy is flawed, it is the stuff of tragedy. In each of his films he has, to one degree or another, lived out that ethic.

Natalie Wood, as Deanie Loomis, has nothing but her heart. Her family is poor, her father is weak and her mother connives. Deanie deeply desires Bud but must remain "unspoiled" (Mom's term) for the marriage that all four parents force the kids to delay. It turns out to be too much for her.

For all the sexual tensions it explores, *Splendor in the Grass* (from Wordsworth's *Intimations of Mortality*) is neither vulgar nor sudsy. Yes, Kazan and Inge use water as Freudian metaphor for sex (Beatty showers, Wood "relaxes" in a hot bath, Beatty debauches under a waterfall, Wood cracks up near a dam), but the emotions in this slowly paced film are clear yet understated, (as befits the repressive era). Above all, there is that stunning concluding sequence in which Wood sees Beatty's ennui and realizes that this would have been her future had she stayed with him. Anybody who has ever attended the wedding of a former flame will feel a familiar painful twinge.

*Splendor in the Grass* is notable for portraying a profound sense of loss, not just of one person for another but for the loss of the sweet innocence of youth and the delicious discovery of a cherished first love.

*DIRECTOR: Elia Kazan WITH: Natalie Wood, Warren Beatty, Pat Hingle*

# Carnal Knowledge (1971)

Saying that *Carnal Knowledge* is a romantic film is like calling *Duck Soup* a war movie. Sure, the elements are there, but they're not where you expect them to be. Even the title warns that this critically hailed work is not about the art of love, but about the act of sex.

And sex is what Jonathan Fuerst (Jack Nicholson) has on his mind throughout the three decades the story covers from 1946 to 1971. Jonathan's name, too, is a pun: Jonathan *first*, which is exactly how he treats every relationship in his life. Although he grows up physically from saddle shoes to crow's feet, he does not age one day emotionally. By the time he realizes how far he has been outdistanced by his friends and social mores, he has descended—presumably irreversibly—into bitter impotence.

Not that he hasn't earned it. After all, he two-times his college roommate (Art Garfunkle) by stealing his girlfriend (Candice Bergen) and "making it" with her before his rommate does. Ten years later he goads his then-wife (Ann-Margret, in an Oscar-nominated performance) first to boredom, then to attempt suicide, by smothering her self–respect with a pageant of his sexism. Finally, in the third decade, he insults the entirety of womankind with a vicious "Ballbusters on Parade" slide show he forces visitors to watch. In the end he must seek the ministrations of a prostitute (Rita Moreno) whose ritualized put-down of women, including herself, is the only way he can get aroused.

Jack Nicholson's Jonathan is sly and supremely manipulative, and just charismatic enough that no one catches on until it's too late. By then he has lost the attractiveness of youth and is just, well, a dirty old man who can't get it up any more.

But a love story? Absolutely, yet in the most cynical way possible: love as the result of playing the game right, but for the wrong reasons, and wondering why it still doesn't work.

As a child of the 40s Jonathan learned to equate sex with power and now uses it to liberate himself from the button-down lawyer's life he has been bred to pursue. But unlike a screen harlot who sleeps her way to the top, Nicholson's satyr has no tragic undertones. This is because men in American society *automatically* succeed and so, to him, sex is not a tool but a weapon. Ironically, it's a weapon he doesn't even like very much; every time he gets laid, Nicholson can't wait to take a shower. He never lingers in bed with a woman and covets only the victory, not the experience.

Despite all this, it is still possible to view *Carnal Knowledge* as a superb love story. Nicholson is constantly seductive, the women in his life (Bergen, Ann-Margret, Cynthia O'Neil, Rita Moreno) are brilliantly defined and expertly portrayed, and there is more passion (albeit dark) between them than can be found in most "relationship" movies that purport to be about love.

*Carnal Knowledge* is either the ultimate in screen sexism or its consummate satire. Its audiences often divide—vehemently—along gender lines. With Jules Feiffer's biting screenplay and Mike Nichols' ascetic direction, the film is a cold dance of betrayal clothed in the trappings of glamor and romance. Long, graceful camera moves and droll, intricate dialogues give *Carnal Knowledge* the look and feel of seduction, when in fact it's only interested in the score.

*DIRECTOR: Mike Nichols WITH: Jack Nicholson, Candice Bergen, Ann-Margret, Rita Moreno*

# A Touch of Class (1973)

Steve: "I have never been unfaithful to my wife . . . in the same city."

Vicki: "Where is your wife now?"

Steve: "Out of town."

With that glib exchange, George Segal and Glenda Jackson begin their bittersweet affair in *A Touch of Class*, a Cary Grant film without Cary Grant. But technically even that isn't really true because, when it was produced, Grant—who had happily retired from the screen in 1966—headed the Fabergé cosmetics empire whose subsidiary, Brut Productions, backed the film.

Certainly the sensibilities of this romantic comedy recall those of Grant's best work: an urbane married man (George Segal) and a secure divorcee (Glenda Jackson) enjoy a carefree European fling only to discover they've unexpectedly fallen in love. Under Melvin Frank's assured direction of his and Jack Rose's brittle, witty script (which was nominated for an Oscar), the film appealed to the adult audiences who had stopped going to the movies in the early 1970s. It also earned Glenda Jackson a second Oscar, rare for a comedy performance.

*A Touch of Class* covers a lot of emotional ground very quickly, and the film's whirlwind pacing mirrors the speed with which Segal and Jackson fall in love. After a series of chance meetings in London, where he's an insurance claims investigator and she's a cut-rate fashion designer (who, by her own admission, "is busy stealing Givenchy's new fall line"), they plot a tryst to follow lunch. "What the hell," Jackson shrugs, "I mean, a girl *has* to eat."

Segal playfully agrees and, shaking her hand too tightly, gushes, "This will do us both a world of good."

"You rather more than I," she says dryly, rubbing her wrist.

But by the time they elude his family, placate a busybody friend (Paul Sorvino), visit Spain and return to London to set up a back-street apartment in Soho, they both realize they're in too deeply to stop. At this point the tension comes not just from traditional sources—Segal's loving but stuffy wife. Jackson's jealous pangs—but from an array of mature emotional conflicts such as irony, self-image, job pressures and even the physical strain of encroaching middle age. It takes Sorvino, who mistakenly believes he introduced them in Spain, to finally ask Segal the big question: "Do you love her enough to give her up?" Several clever plot twists later, Segal answers it.

Coming between the experimental nude period of the late sixties and the frat-house humor of the late sixties the tone of *A Touch of Class* is occasionally out of place. Its studio-slick photography, lush music, and breezy pace are reminiscent of Hollywood's frothy romantic comedies, while its content (happy adulterers) marks it for a newer, more libidinous age. But these are just growing pains, not debits, and the film surmounts most of them. The sheer giddiness in lovers Jackson and Segal having a pillow fight, their crisp after-sex sparring match and their cheeky, confident immorality are hard to resist.

Alas, it was also hard to duplicate; Jackson, Segal, Sorvino, and writer-director Frank tried it again six years later with *Lost and Found*, a romantic comedy about a college tenure fight. Like an affair of the heart, *A Touch of Class* proved just as impossible to recapture as it was to forget.

*DIRECTOR: Melvin Frank WITH: George Segal, Glenda Jackson, Paul Sorvino*

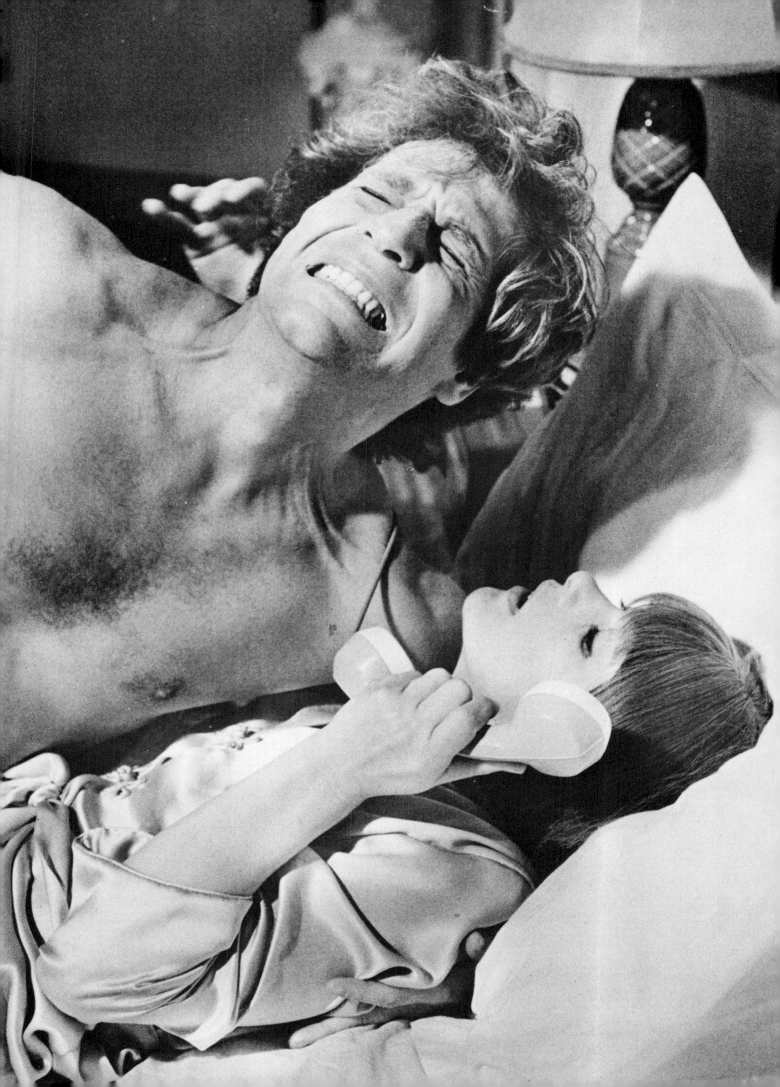

# The Way We Were (1973)

What Robert Redford brings to many of his films are his good looks and a sense that, underneath, he is a man trying to break out of the limitations placed on him by others because of those looks. Nowhere is that more apparent than in this doomed love story between Hubbell Gardiner (Redford) and Katie Morosky (Barbra Streisand). In Arthur Laurents' script (based on his novel) it is Hubbell who is given the clear vision to see that this relationship is never going to work, and yet who lacks the gumption to prevent its being played out to the bitter end.

In the college flashback scenes in the 1930s, we see both what attracts these two to each other and why it can never be. Katie is the head of the campus Young Communist League and an outspoken pacifist. Her closest relationship seems to be with Frankie (James Woods in an early role), and it is strictly Party-line. Hubbell is a well-heeled WASP given to writing stories about Pife's victories coming so easily for him.

What seems to attract them to each other is the ways in which they are different. For all his protests to the contrary, Hubbell is looking for a life of no heavy lifting. His authorship of a novel provides him both an entrée into Hollywood and an excuse to stop work on his second novel. For Katie, Hollywood means selling out. Worse, *everything* is political for her, while Hubbell thinks politics is merely a good subject for jokes among his friends. He is amazed at her penchant for political talk. "I don't know how you do it," he says in wonder.

"I don't know how you can't," she replies.

This lack of commonality between them—and their inability to change—ensures the failure of their relationship. "When you love someone," he tells her, "you go deaf, dumb, and blind." But she was always more interested in what she might turn him into rather than who he actually was. Indeed, beyond those surface good looks and his writing, she never really sees him at all.

For Robert Redford, *The Way We Were* made him one of the romantic icons of the decade. Already a star from *Butch Cassidy and the Sundance Kid* (1969), he hadn't really appeared as a romantic lead since *Barefoot in the Park* (1967). The film also further cemented his relationship with director Sydney Pollack. Among their other films together are *This Property Is Condemned* (1966), *Jeremiah Johnson* (1972), *Three Days of the Condor* (1976), *The Electric Horseman* (1979), *Out of Africa* (1985) and *Havana* (1990).

Barbra Streisand had been a major star since her 1968 Oscar-winning debut in *Funny Girl*. Her Katie struck a chord with those who had reached for a romantic possibility that was ultimately beyond their grasp. Singing the Oscar-winning title song didn't hurt either.

A note should be made about the historical background of the film, which covers the late thirties to early fifties. The key political issue that eventually destroys their marriage is the Hollywood blacklist, where those who had signed the wrong petitions or joined the wrong organizations were declared "un-American" and lost their jobs. The final version of the film cuts much of that material out, omitting any implication that Hubbell has betrayed his friends by "naming names" to save his neck.

The filmmakers were lost on the little things as well as the big things. One of the famous scenes in the film is the "Marx Brothers party" for Hubbell's friend J.J. (Bradford Dillman). Everyone is dressed as Groucho or Harpo (with no Chico in evidence), and a movie poster hung as a decoration advertises the film *Love Happy*. The only problem is that the scene is set in 1947, and *Love Happy* wouldn't be made for another two years.

Audiences didn't care. For all the omissions and inaccuracies they preferred remembering this as "the way we were."

*DIRECTOR: Sydney Pollack WITH: Barbra Streisand, Robert Redford, Bradford Dillman, James Woods, Lois Chiles, Patrick O'Neal*

# Annie Hall (1977)

After relating the old joke about why the man keeps his brother who thinks he's a chicken, Alvy Singer (Woody Allen) tells us, "I guess that's pretty much how I feel about relationships. You know, they're totally irrational and crazy and absurd, but I guess we keep going through it because most of us need the eggs."

Allen's Oscar-winning romantic comedy—it took Best Picture, Best Director, Best Screenplay, and Best Actress—almost wasn't a romantic comedy at all. Originally entitled *Anhedonia*, it was to be Alvy's ruminations on his life and times. As film editor Ralph Rosenblum relates in his book with Robert Karen, *When the Shooting Stops . . .* , the movie as we know it took shape in the editing room as Allen shifted the focus to relationships, and especially his love for Annie Hall, played by Allen's ex-girlfriend Diane Keaton.

Popularly assumed to be autobiographical (Keaton's real name is Diane Hall), *Annie Hall* gives us the rise and fall of a relationship but with the perspective of hindsight. We know right from the beginning that Alvy and Annie have broken up, and that colors the way we see them. In many ways, *Annie Hall* is about the process of reconciling oneself to a love affair after it is over.

We see it all, from the coy conversations to the petty fights, from the decision to move in together to the decision to break apart. Alvy tells us how he keeps sifting the pieces of the relationship through his mind, and that's exactly how we get them.

There are scenes that are vintage Allen: Annie invites Alvy over for a glass of wine after they first meet and Allen provides us with subtitles revealing what the characters are *really* thinking while they babble small talk; after their first breakup Alvy is fixed up with a spacy reporter (Shelley Duvall) from *Rolling Stone*, who describes sex with him as a "Kafkaesque experience."

These intellectual forays are the reasons that Allen has his devoted legion of fans. Yet *Annie Hall* reached out beyond the hard-core Allen addicts and it was those quieter moments that tapped into something larger than his patented brand of New York neuroticism:

• The First Kiss: Alvy and Annie are walking down a street on their way to dinner on their first date, and he suddenly stops her and suggests they kiss. When she is startled, he explains that since they never kissed before he'll "never know when to make the right move or anything." By taking the pressure off the moment, he suggests, "We'll digest our food better."

• The Breakup: Alvy and Annie are sitting on a plane each realizing their relationship is over and wondering how they'll break it to the other. Finally Alvy has the perfect metaphor, "A relationship is like a shark. It has to constantly move forward or it dies. And I think what we've got on our hands is a dead shark."

• The Rebound Date: Alvy takes a woman out to a beach house in the Hamptons and attempts to recreate a comically romantic moment with Annie by exhibiting fright at a live lobster. When he tells her that he's nervous because he gave up smoking sixteen years ago, she looks at him blankly, and says, "Are you joking or what?"

At the end he and Annie are reconciled—as friends, not lovers. Perhaps the most autobiographical comment in the film comes when Alvy is rehearsing the first play he has written, which features a scene remarkably like his breakup with Annie, only with him *winning* her hand. Turning to us in the audience, he explains, "You're always trying to get things to come out perfect in art, because it's real difficult in life."

*DIRECTOR: Woody Allen WITH: Woody Allen, Diane Keaton, Tony Roberts, Colleen Dewhurst, Christopher Walken, Paul Simon, Carol Kane, Janet Margolin, Shelley Duvall*

111

# CHAPTER SIX

# Love and Marriage

*The way Hollywood avoids making movies about married life, you'd think it was out of fashion to tie the knot. These next films show husbands and wives who like each other as well as love each other, often through some pretty tough times.*

# The Thin Man (1934)

This mystery-comedy series based on the popular novel by Dashiell Hammett is notable for three things. First, and perhaps most important, it showed that fun and romance don't have to end when the wedding bells stop ringing. Unlike most romantic comedies, the *Thin Man* stories didn't have to rely on the couple making or renewing their vows. The movies let the *mystery* carry the burden of the plot, as it did in Dashiell Hammett's original novel. This lets Nick and Nora Charles (William Powell, Myrna Loy) remain happily married throughout the entire series. Apparently the couple that solves murders together, stays together.

Watching the films today, it's easy to see why they remain popular, in spite of the creaky trappings of the plots. (Well before the series ended, other movie detectives had stopped summoning all the suspects into a room for the exposure of the murderer.) Nick's raffish charm is the perfect complement to Nora's sophisticated wit. He's an ex–police detective trying to put his past behind him, while she is utterly captivated by it. At a Christmas party filled with reporters, drunks, murder suspects and ex-cons, she embraces him and says, "Oh Nicky, I love you because you know such lovely people."

They are both quick with the wisecrack, but it is something that serves to unite them rather than an excuse for taking shots at each other. Theirs is a relationship built on trust. When Nora opens a bedroom door and finds Nick embracing a beautiful young woman, he grimaces at her as if daring her to make something of it. Her response is simply to make a face back at him, and then see if there's anything she can do to help. The idea that Nick could ever be unfaithful to her just doesn't exist.

The second reason that the series is important is that it created the legendary screen team of William Powell and Myrna Loy, who would appear in twelve more movies together. They were so identified as a movie couple that when Powell soloed in *The Senator Was Indiscreet* (1947), his oft-referred–to wife back home is revealed in the film's final scene to be none other than Loy.

And third, alone of the romantic comedies of the '30s, it spawned a series of sequels. Instead of wondering what became of this couple at the final fadeout, we were allowed to watch Nick and Nora Charles in five more films—through her pregnancy in *After the Thin Man* (1936) and increasing domesticity in *Another Thin Man* (1939), *Shadow of the Thin Man* (1941), *The Thin Man Goes Home* (1944) and *Song of the Thin Man* (1947). (Incidentally, *The Thin Man* of the first film is *not* Nick, but the first murder victim.)

*The Thin Man* and its sequels are tied to the cycle of screwball comedies of the period not only through the casting of Powell and Loy (whose credits, together and apart, include such films as *Libeled Lady*, *My Man Godfrey*, *Double Wedding* and *Too Hot to Handle*) but also through the presence of Asta, the wire-haired fox terrier who appeared in all six films and became increasingly domestic himself. He also appears as Mr. Smith, the subject of the "custody" battle in *The Awful Truth* (1937), and as the bone-stealing George of *Bringing Up Baby* (1938). The overlapping casting added to the sense that all these films shared the same world of romantic comedy, regardless of what happened to be going on in any one particular movie.

When Nick and Nora appeared in their final film (with a young Dean Stockwell as Nicky, Jr.), they had made the transition from newlyweds to being an old married couple. And they were still very much in love.

*DIRECTOR: W. S. Van Dyke II WITH: William Powell, Myrna Loy, Maureen O'Sullivan, Nat Pendleton, Cesar Romero*

# The Awful Truth (1937)

Can a married couple show their love for each other by laughter as well as kissing? That's what Cary Grant and Irene Dunne do in *The Awful Truth*—to bad they have to get divorced to realize it.

The film's premise is both playful and naughty: a marital misunderstanding forces the prideful Grant and Dunne into a divorce that neither wants. To settle mutual scores, he spoons with a socialite (Molly Lamont) while she woos a rube (Ralph Bellamy), each doing everything possible to foul up the other's chances. They finally realize that they are still in love, at which time they decide to try again.

*The Awful Truth* is not only one of the most effervescent comedies ever to come out of Hollywood, it is also a deft end run around the strict Production Code Office, which had recently been empowered as the industry's censorship bureau. The Code stood against everything that was even remotely adult in motion pictures—yet adultery was exactly what this film happened to be about. Its secret was that it did it with humor.

Made three years after *It Happened One Night* began the era of screwball comedy, *The Awful Truth* confirmed the genre and began new careers for its two leads. Irene Dunne had appeared in dramatic films such as *Showboat* and *Back Street;* her only previous comedy had been *Theodora Goes Wild*. Cary Grant, although a star, was not yet established as a comic lead. *The Awful Truth* changed all that.

For starters, it was affectionate. Grant and Dunne are so obviously made for each other—and just as obviously not made for their interim dates—that the comedy comes from watching them obnoxiously look out for each other's best interests. When Dunne, visiting a night club, gets a load of a floozie whom Grant is dating, she appraises her with "I guess it was easier for her to change her name than for a whole family to change theirs." Similarly, when Grant crashes Dunne's operatic recital (he suspects that her singing teacher is a co-respondent) and tumbles off a chair, Dunne wryly laughs at him in mid-aria, disguising her chortle as part of the song.

Their barbed banter continues throughout; the more they swap insults, the more they know they are in love. For example, Grant chides the bon vivant Dunne for wanting to run off to Oklahoma City with the drab Bellamy, with, "And if it should get dull you can always go over to Tulsa for the weekend." And she gets even by gloating when he is injured by a collapsing piano, "Did it hurt you much? Just the one hand?"

If they spar with each other they spare nothing on interlopers: Ralph Bellamy (in the first of what came to be known as "Ralph Bellamy roles") is mocked for being a hick: "I'm very lucky," he tells a bemused Grant. "Y'know what they call me back home?" to which Grant sneers, "I can guess." Alex D'Arcy, the singing teacher, is pummeled offscreen by Grant while Dunne's sarcastic Aunt Patsy (Cecil Cunningham) reports, "Somebody's cleaning up in there"; later when Grant chases D'Arcy out of the apartment, Cunningham announces, "They forgot to touch second!"

Director Leo McCarey (who won an Oscar) and screenwriter Vena Delmar revel in putting their characters into embarrassing situations knowing that they are agile enough to avoid disaster. But they saved their ultimate joke for the Code Office: Stranded in separate rooms in a resort house awaiting their divorce to become final, Dunne and Grant reunite to resume their romance at the stroke of midnight. But technically at this point they are no longer married.

Leave it to McCarey, Delmar, Grant and Dunne to have everybody put one past the censors.

*DIRECTOR: Leo McCarey WITH: Cary Grant, Irene Dunne, Ralph Bellamy*

# His Girl Friday (1940)

When director Howard Hawks remade Ben Hecht and Charles MacArthur's classic newspaper comedy *The Front Page* as *His Girl Friday* in 1940, he changed it from a buddy yarn into a love story straight out of the tabloids.

*The Front Page* is about how conniving newspaper editor Walter Burns will do anything to keep his star reporter, Hildy Johnson, from getting married and leaving town. In the original play, Hildy is a guy, and the whole tale is about male bonding in an almost exclusively male profession; the women who do appear are a cleaning lady, a battle ax, a virgin and a whore.

Hawks changed all that. He saw that *The Front Page* was really a love story between "the journalese twins" and discovered—supposedly settling a party wager—that it could work even better if Hildy Johnson was a woman.

Thus did Rosalind Russell come to play Hildy, who in this adaptation wasn't only the best writer Walter (Cary Grant) ever hired, she was also his ex-wife. As the now-female Hildy discovers while doing Walter the favor of covering convicted killer Earl Williams's daring jailbreak, she's still in love with him. More precisely, she's still in love with the excitement that swirls around him.

*His Girl Friday*'s second, perhaps equally powerful, love story is the one between Hildy Johnson and journalism. For not only does Hildy fall back in love with Walter and ditch her fiancé, the colorless Bruce Baldwin (Ralph Bellamy), she falls back in love with journalism and re-ups with *The Morning Post*. The other reporters in the Criminal Courts Building press room taunt her that her romance with journalism is bound to go unrequited. But even if it does, it sure beats living in Albany with Ralph Bellamy.

*His Girl Friday* is an endlessly watchable movie. Hawks's best films deal with people who are good at doing their jobs, and here he gets to make a movie full of them—not just the two leads but also a supporting cast of expert reporters played by Hollywood's best character actors (Cliff Edwards, Porter Hall, Roscoe Karns, Billy Gilbert, Gene Lockhart, and Ernest Truex, among others). As would come true in the best ensemble television sitcoms (*Taxi, Cheers, Mary Tyler Moore*), *His Girl Friday* excels when everybody is evenly matched. Every time Hildy and Walter hurl insults, double-cross each other, exchange disparaging remarks, or try to swindle their own colleagues, they are also thoroughly enjoying themselves, and everyone knows it. The fact that they also recapture the killer, expose a corrupt political machine, and send Bruce back to Albany only proves that Walter was right about Hildy all along. So, obviously, when he once again proposes to her and she—however much she resents him and his ways—accepts, we know that they are really made for each other.

For the most part, *His Girl Friday* is a remarkably progressive film. Hildy is just as strong as Walter, she's good at what she does, and—except for some momentary tears of frustration near the end—she matches the males point for point. To certain feminist observers, of course, this means that she's defining herself in male terms, but in 1940 it was the highest honor a female character could be accorded. Whether Hildy and Walter will keep on fighting, and will live forever in a mutually sadistic relationship, is something for shrinks to decide, not lovers.

*DIRECTOR: Howard Hawks WITH: Cary Grant, Rosalind Russell, Ralph Bellamy*

# The Palm Beach Story (1942)

One of the most delightful rewards of the renewed interest in movie director Preston Sturges was rediscovering this nutty movie from the end of Hollywood's great cycle of screwball comedies. It's only *after* the final fadeout of most Hollywood romances, *The Palm Beach Story* tells us, that the real romantic adventure begins.

The film starts with what seems to be the end of another film. We see Joel McCrea and Claudette Colbert overcoming all odds in a photo-finish race to the altar. He's getting into his tails in the car, while she's racing across town in a bridal gown. Meanwhile there's a maid who keeps passing out and *another* character played by Colbert who has been tied up and locked in a closet. As the wedding ceremony begins, the camera pulls back and the words "And they lived happily ever after" appear. This is quickly followed by the words "Or did they?"

The movie proper begins five years later, when Tom Jeffers (McCrea) and his wife Gerry (Colbert) are up to their ears in bills in their spacious Park Avenue apartment. He is an inventor who lacks backers, while her major skills seem to be shopping and looking fashionable. Tom and Gerry (their names obviously inspired by the cartoon cat and mouse) are in trouble.

Gerry decides that she is "useless as a wife" and would actually be helping Tom by getting out of his life. She thinks Tom would be able to get ahead on his own, and meanwhile she would be able to find a "good provider" for herself.

Since he won't bust up their marriage voluntarily, she runs off in order to force him to strike out on his own. Instead he is soon in hot pursuit. On one level the film is about how far an attractive woman can get on nothing more than wit and beauty. "You have no idea what a long-legged gal can do without doing anything," she tells Tom.

Gerry depends on what she calls "the look"—those glances that men have been giving her since she was a teenager—and the film justifies her reliance. Rescuers crawl out of the woodwork, from the Texas Wienie King who pays all their bills, to the Ale & Quail Club, who let her on their private car on a departing train, to the wealthy John D. Hackensacker III (Rudy Vallee), who offers her clothes, food, a roof over her head and a life of unending ease; but none of these men is really much of a threat.

Upon Tom's arrival at Hackensacker's Palm Beach estate, Gerry introduces him as her "brother" Captain McGlue. When Hackensacker's sister, the Princess Centamilla (Mary Astor), is attracted to Tom, Gerry sees this wealthy couple as the solution to all their problems. Yet *The Palm Beach Story* rejects such cynicism, questioning whether trading love for comfort generates any lasting guarantee of either condition.

In what has to be considered one of the oddest love scenes in Hollywood history, Tom and Gerry spend the night together and rediscover the love that brought them close in the first place. Meanwhile, down below the bedroom window, Hackensacker is crooning, "Good night sweetheart, though I'm not beside you/Good night sweetheart, still my love will guide you." Indeed, it does guide her, right back into the arms of her husband.

If Sturges is making any point here it is that Tom and Gerry's marriage was on the rocks because they were neglecting each other. Love will get you to the point of "and they lived happily ever after" but then it's up to the couple to make their love work.

Still, *The Palm Beach Story* is a movie, and thus requires a happy ending. It's got one, and it's a lulu. Hackensacker and the Princess are disappointed they've lost Gerry and Tom, but they are delighted to learn that *both* of them have identical twin siblings. (So *that's* who the girl in the closet was!) The movie ends with a triple wedding, and the same question about what's going to happen to these looney lovers after the words "The End."

*DIRECTOR: Preston Sturges WITH: Joel McCrea, Claudette Colbert, Rudy Vallee, Mary Astor*

# The Best Years of Our Lives (1946)

The horror of World War II destroyed more than Europe and Japan, it also ruptured the American family forever. Not only were hundreds of thousands of husbands, fathers and sons killed or wounded, but an equal number of wives, mother and daughters changed in their absence. For as much as everybody in America 1945 assumed they would all take up where they had left off in 1941, the truth was that life would never be the same again.

Women had learned to work outside the home; many held jobs that the returning GIs were told they would be entitled to have back. While they were grateful for peace, women also resented being replaced. Men, too, were restless; after Normandy or Bataan, the prospect of stepping back behind a drug store soda fountain held little appeal. The often-difficult readjustment of veterans and their families became the subject for Samuel Goldwyn's 1946 production *The Best Years of Our Lives*, which William Wyler—himself an injured veteran—directed.

Three stories on this theme intertwine: Fredric March is the middle-aged banker for whom home and office cannot match the thrill of battle; Dana Andrews is the poor boy to whom the army gave status and a uniform, but no job skills; and Harold Russell—who had actually lost both hands in an explosion—is the disabled soldier who now feels unworthy of his family and fiancée.

Of the justifiably memorable scenes in *The Best Years of Our Lives*, those that spotlight domestic life remain the most moving. Chief among them is March's reunion with wife Myrna Loy. Arriving unexpectedly, he is greeted at the door by their children and quickly gains their silence. From the kitchen Loy asks, "Who was that at the door?" and, as the music becomes softly restrained, she turns, asking, "Peggy? Rob? What was . . ." then senses her husband's presence. They meet and embrace as so many other couples did, after VI Day—among them director Wyler and his own wife.

Russell's homecoming is far less joyous. As he waves goodbye to his friends in the taxi, his parents' eyes are drawn to his hooks. Later he will explain his anguish to Wilma, his faithful girlfriend, and give her a harsh demonstration of how helpless he is without them—just in case she still dares to love him.

Dana Andrews' wounds are to his ego; he suspects that his wife (Virginia Mayo) was unfaithful while he was away. Once his discharge pay is spent, so is her love for him. Crushed, he is forced to beg for work in a town whose provincialism reminds him of his shortcomings. Were it not for meeting Peggy (Thersa Wright), Fredric March's daughter, Andrews would be as ruined as the junked bombers he visits in the airplane graveyard—another sequence that has etched the film into America's collective memory.

In adapting Mackinley Kantor's difficult novel to the screen, Robert E. Sherwood used love as a device for healing. The film's mature themes met with opposition; the strict Production Code office objected to intimations of adultery, home wrecking, disability, alcoholism and unhappiness among returning veterans. As usual, the public's enthusiastic approval showed that the censors were out of touch and *The Best Years of Our Lives* became the most successful film since *Gone With the Wind*. It won seven Oscars (two for Russell) including Best Picture, and sped the movies toward acknowledging that life in the United States was no longer solely the stuff that dreams were made of.

*DIRECTOR: William Wyler WITH: Fredric March, Myrna Loy, Dana Andrews, Harold Russell*

# Adam's Rib (1949)

When it comes to "battle of the sexes" films, *Adam's Rib* is in a class by itself. Written by the husband and wife team of Ruth Gordon and Garson Kanin, and starring Spencer Tracy and Katharine Hepburn as married lawyers on opposite sides of a case, it is a film that seems as fresh now as the day it was released.

Part of it is because of what we've learned about the actors' relationship (largely from Kanin's memoir *Tracy and Hepburn*) in subsequent years, and part of it is the special magic the two wove in most of their nine films together.

The famous story about Tracy and Hepburn's first meeting involved MGM's pairing of the stars for *Woman of the Year*. Bumping into each other by chance, they were introduced by their mutual friend, director Joseph Mankiewicz. "I fear I may be too tall for you, Mr. Tracy," Hepburn said. "Don't worry, he'll cut you down to size," interjected Mankiewicz. (For many years the line was attributed to Tracy, but Hepburn has since set the record straight.)

In *Adam's Rib*, Tracy plays Adam Bonner, the attorney assigned to prosecute Doris Attinger (Judy Holliday) for having shot and wounded her philandering husband, Warren (Tom Ewell). Convinced that the law would excuse a man in the reverse situation, Adam's wife Amanda (Hepburn) signs on as Doris's defender. Her case, she explains, "is based on the proposition that persons of the female sex should be dealt with before the law as the equals of persons of the male sex."

She's right, of course, and she knows it. While she is eager to try the case, Adam dreads it, knowing that in spite of Doris's actions and confession, there will be no joy in prosecution. Adam and Amanda's battle of wits in the courtroom is hilarious, with Amanda becoming increasingly ruthless in undercutting her husband before the jury.

What's special about this couple is that they really care about each other. Their problem is that the case brings out their competitive sides, and they find they can't turn off the arguing, even in the bedroom. Each tries, but they're out of sync.

"We've had our little differences and I've always tried to see your point of view," says a visibly angry Adam, "but this time you've got me stumped, baby." Amanda is reduced to tears, and he mocks her for turning on "the juice," but moments later he calms down and tries to reconcile with her. Now *she's* the angry one, and won't have any of it.

She wins the case, but Adam threatens her as Doris had threatened her husband, and Amanda is forced to concede that Adam was right. (Adam then takes a bite out of his gun, made of licorice.) Each has now won an argument, but their marriage is in tatters. The confrontation that works so well in the courtroom is a disaster for a marriage, which thrives on compromise and cooperation. The two lawyers meet with their accountant to go over their taxes, and now it is Adam who turns on the juice—to melt Amanda's heart and win her back. He's a man who's big enough to cry, and even more important, he's adopted *her* tactic to preserve their marriage.

When he shows her that he really can turn it on and off, she says that he has proved *her* point: that men and women should be equal because there really is no difference between them. He gets her to admit that there might be a "little difference" after all.

As they retire to their marital bed and a renewed commitment, he can only add, "Vive la difference!"

*DIRECTOR: George Cukor WITH: Spencer Tracy, Katharine Hepburn, David Wayne, Tom Ewell, Judy Holliday, Jean Hagen*

# A Star Is Born (1954)

Hollywood has an axiom: Never make movies about movies.

Somehow the problems of a town full of beautiful, talented, rich people just don't appeal to the world at large, and those who think otherwise are bound to fail. Oh, there have been some successes—Brackett and Wilder's *Sunset Boulevard* and Minnelli's *The Bad and the Beautiful* are two—but others, such as *The Big Picture* (1989), belong more to movie buffs than wide audiences.

Then there is *A Star Is Born*, the 1954 film that was as hopeful, yet as doomed, as the story it tells of one Hollywood star (Judy Garland) on the rise who loves another (James Mason) who is on the decline both professionally and personally.

Originally filmed in 1937 with Janet Gaynor and Fredric March, that first version was itself inspired by *What Price Hollywood?* (1932). Both films were directed by George Cukor. Each, it is said, chronicled the tragic and grotesque later life of John Barrymore, although the film industry has proved that it has enough cruelty to fuel several similar scenarios.

One of them belonged to Norman Maine (Mason), whose pictures for mogul Oliver Niles (Charles Bickford) have been faring badly, largely because of Maine's increasingly unstable behavior.

At the same time, Maine discovers a fresh new talent in Esther Blodgett (Garland), whom Niles signs to a contract. With a name change to Vicki Lester and a lucky break in a hit musical, Lester quickly overtakes Maine at the box office. They also fall deeply in love. When Maine drinks himself into complete ruin Lester, who loves him more than ever, resolves to forsake her career to care for him. Shamed at hearing this, Maine commits suicide. Only with great effort does Esther return to public view, delivering one of the movies' greatest curtain lines: "Ladies and Gentlemen, this is Mrs. Norman Maine!"

Although it is, of course, a story about the caprices of stardom, the soul of *A Star Is Born* is the unfailing love between Norman and Esther.

"I destroy everything I touch," Norman warns her, but she desperately loves him anyway, and so persists in trying to save him from his own behavior. Finally she has to admit that she has failed: "You don't know what it's like watching somebody you love just crumble away bit by bit, day by day, in front of your eyes, and stand there helpless," she confesses to Niles. "Love isn't enough. I thought it was."

Esther's devotion to Norman is total, but for thirty years her exact reasons remained a mystery—key scenes, which might justify the intensity of their bond, seemed to be missing from the picture. The answer lay locked in Warner Bros. vaults.

When it was released in 1954, *A Star Is Born* ran just over three hours. Complaints from the theater forced Warner Bros. to cut half an hour to allow an extra showing per day. The deleted footage—long thought to be lost—contained character scenes that explained the depth of the Norman–Esther relationship. In 1983 film historian Ronald Haver painstakingly located and inserted the footage; the result was a revelation.

In the restored film James Mason is seen to have given one of the screen's great performances as a frustrated Shakespearean actor forced to waste his talent in films. Garland, controlled and mature, shows off her (real-life) wit, not just tears. And we see more of their delicate early interplay before tragedy sets in.

It is also a remarkably intimate film despite its setting. For all its innovative color styling, wise use of early CinemaScope (completely lost on home video), nuanced performances and sharp writing (by Moss Hart), *A Star Is Born* is not only about the movies, it's about people and their dreams. The characters may be bigger than life, but the emotions they display touch us all.

*DIRECTOR: George Cukor WITH: Judy Garland, James Mason, Charles Bickford, Jack Carson*

# Two for the Road (1967)

They say that when a person dies, his life flashes in front of him. According to *Two for the Road*, when a marriage dies, *its* life flashes in front of the man and woman who used to share it. At least, that's the case set forth by this stylish, intriguing jigsaw puzzle of a movie.

Joanna and Mark Wallace (Audrey Hepburn and Albert Finney) have traveled Europe every summer for the twelve years since they first met when he was an architectural student and she sang in a girls' chorus. They mark the years by their transport (from hitchhiking to a Mercedes) and also by their baggage (backpacks at the beginning, adulterous affairs toward the end). After a while the trips, like the events of their marriage, run into one another until there is no logic left, only ennui.

Screenwriter Frederic Raphael (who won an Oscar for writing *Darling* in 1965) hopscotches through time in *Two for the Road*. At one moment he follows Hepburn and Finney's fresh-faced romance, then he cuts to a later tour with William Daniels, Eleanor Bron, and their Child from Hell, then to an equally disastrous stay at an unaffordable French inn. The picturesque setting belies the nitty-gritty of their relationship as they realize that even though they're in love, they also gnaw on each other's nerves.

That checkerboard texture is key for Raphael and director Stanley Donen, whose facile technique—like the Wallaces' marriage—looks far cooler than it is. Marriage, after all, is built on incident, and as Joanna and Mark try to sort out the incidents, so does the viewer.

Like marriage counseling, *Two for the Road* takes effort. Much of it involves seeing through the glib dialogue ("I'm so happy I'm so happy" or "I still want a child, I just don't want *that* child"). At other times Hepburn and Finney resort to "the cutes"—lovey-dovey facial expressions actors use to con the audience through illogical script moments.

Yet the overall effect is to sketch, with more precision than most films dare attempt, the gamut of joys and sorrows of modern marriage. Fortunately, the scale tips toward happiness: For every hotel with bad room service, there are ten gorgeous sunsets. For every car that blows up, there is a gleeful picnic in bed. For every case of beach sunburn, there is a dip in a cool resort swimming pool. All of these are mixed and matched with the dedication of two people searching for the good times and discovering that they far outweigh the bad.

At three points in *Two for the Road* Hepburn and Finney see older couples and swap this dialogue:

"What kind of people just sit like that without a word to say to each other?"

"Married people."

As their back-and-forth travails offer insight into their own marriage, they begin using the couplet on themselves. Along with continually exchanging the epithets "bitch" and "bastard" (such as when she, in a running gag, keeps finding the passport that he keeps losing), it is clear that Finney and Hepburn love each other. But it is also clear that they test that love as often as they prove it. *Two for the Road* is as painful as a memory book and its edges give cuts that are just as nasty. But it also chronicles a marriage as few motion pictures ever have.

*DIRECTOR: Stanley Donen WITH: Audrey Hepburn, Albert Finney, Eleanor Bron, William Daniels*

# Pete 'n' Tillie (1972)

Although he had built a solid dramatic reputation with such films as *Lonely Are the Brave* (1962), *Fail-Safe* (1964), and *Mirage* (1962), Walter Matthau's star was turned forever toward comedy with his Oscar-winning performance in Billy Wilder's 1966 *The Fortune Cookie*.

Matthau always resented this. Even though he wryly called himself "the Ukrainian Cary Grant," he pined for the greater satisfaction of serious films.

*Pete 'n' Tillie* accorded him both. A comedy-drama that follows the courtship, marriage, tragedy, and re-courtship of Pete Seltzer (Matthau) and Tillie Schlaine (Carol Burnett), it owes a debt to George Stevens' *Penny Serenade* (1941) in that it, too, expertly pulls audiences through a remarkable number of highs and lows without dropping the emotional ball.

The saga of Pete and Tillie starts pleasantly enough in the sixties, when the "ageless" (one of the film's best running gags) Geraldine Page pairs them at a party. Several dates and dozens of wisecracks later, Pete asks Tillie up to his place "for some heavy breathing" and she agrees. Six months and much heavy breathing later she puts her foot down: "Honeymoon's over; time to get married."

The extraordinary story that follows is played through Mr. and Mrs. Seltzer and their menagerie of friends. Barry Nelson, married to Page, has always been fond of Tillie. So has René Auberjonois' gay decorator (a stock role inventively handled).

Because *Pete 'n' Tillie* covers ten years, it is necessarily told in fragmented style, but Julius J. Epstein's brittle script and Martin Ritt's well-paced direction expertly stay the emotional course. And *Pete 'n' Tillie is* emotional in mature, realistic, highly textured ways, which accounts for its appeal beyond the facile romantic comedy that it first appears to be.

For example, even though we are inclined to think Matthau is charmingly funny and Burnett is his comic match, her reserve in their first scenes perfectly sets up their futures—he plays, she observes, then keeps her own counsel. Later this strength serves them both well, especially when their son (Lee H. Montgomery) falls seriously ill in the film's difficult second act. By the time Pete and Tillie reconcile, they have done more than fall back in love; they have rebuilt a bond that will sustain them for the rest of their lives.

After *Pete 'n' Tillie* the drama bug was stronger in Matthau than ever. Over the next two years he quickly made the crime thrillers *Charley Varrick* (1973), *The Laughing Policeman* (1973), and *The Taking of Pelham 1–2–3* (1974), all of which—despite solid work—just reminded audiences of how much they wanted Matthau to make them laugh. With *The Sunshine Boys* (1975) he remembered, too, and has never forgotten.

*DIRECTOR: Martin Ritt WITH: Walter Matthau, Carol Burnett, Geraldine Page, Barry Nelson*

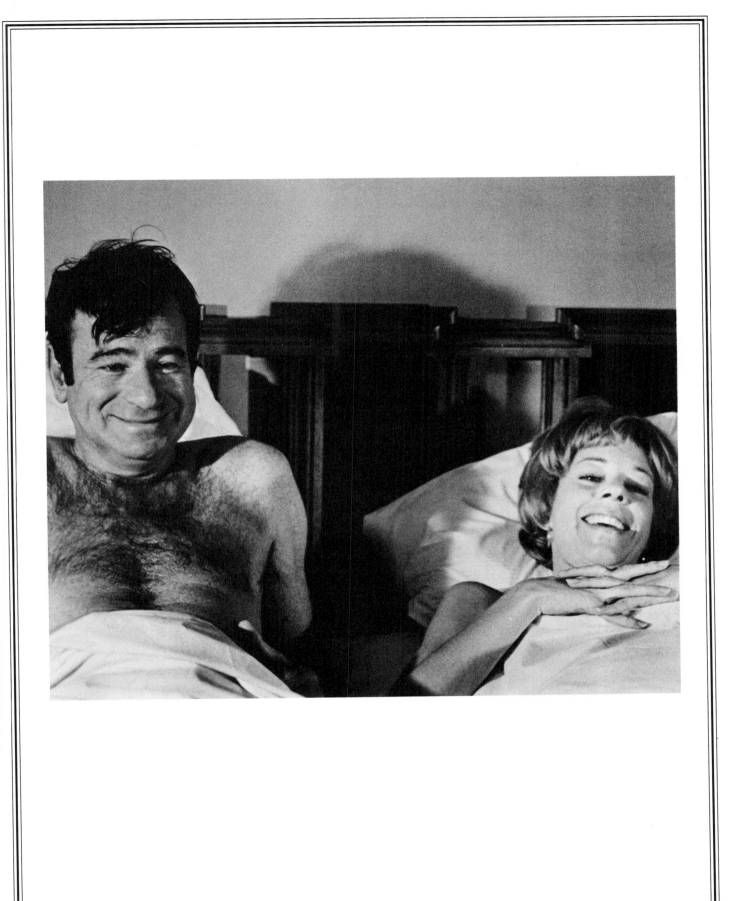

# Strangers in the Night

*Love isn't always pretty, but in these films it's pretty entertaining. From foggy moors and fetid jungles to the world of* film noir *and steamy summer nights, these are romances of the psyche as well as of the heart.*

# King Kong (1933)

# Bride of Frankenstein (1935)

In a way, many of the older horror films are romances, not only because of the intentionally gothic and mysterious atmosphere but also because unrequited love is a constant theme. Even *Dr. Jekyll and Mr. Hyde* has both sides of this split personality looking for love.

Back in the days when something advertised as a "horror movie" didn't bring to mind a guy in a hockey mask chopping up horny teenagers, it was possible to shed a tear over the fate of the monsters and madmen who appeared on the screen. Most of them really didn't deserve it. Indeed, some of them were only fighting loneliness.

*King Kong* (1933) has lots of action and special effects as two adventurers (Bruce Cabot, Robert Armstrong) discover and capture the giant ape of the title. Kong may be a gigantic, savage animal living in a prehistoric jungle, but he isn't bad, only misunderstood. If he had his druthers he'd simply settle down with Ann Redman (Fay Wray) in his little hideaway.

Instead he is captured and taken to New York, where he is displayed in chains before gawking theatergoers. Is it any wonder he runs off with Ann and climbs the Empire State Building? He is finally shot down in a spectacular sequence, credited to codirectors Merian C. Cooper and Ernest B. Schoedsack, and special effects wizard Willis O'Brien.

The final verdict, though, is not that Kong was brought down by superior firepower, but that "'twas beauty killed the beast." It was his love for Ann that made him vulnerable, and the impossibility of a relationship between a gigantic ape and a city girl that is the tragedy of *Kong*.

Another monster brought low through unrequited love was the creation of Dr. Frankenstein (Colin Clive), who brings his original creature (from 1931's *Frankenstein*) back to life in *The Bride of Frankenstein*. Believing the monster (Boris Karloff) to be lonely, he plans to create a mate: another corpse reanimated in his laboratory.

Meanwhile we get to see that Frankenstein's monster is really just a poor soulless creature who, like the rest of us, only wants companionship. In one of the most memorable sequences of the film, the monster is taken into the humble cottage of a blind man (O. P. Heggie), who teaches him to drink and smoke. Unable to see the monster, he welcomes him as a friend.

The unveiling of the "bride" is the climactic moment of the movie. Played by Elsa Lanchester (who was also Mary Shelley in the opening prologue), she is nearly as hideous as the monster, sporting a beehive hairdo with lightning streaks running up the sides. Perhaps this will be the monster's companion and cure him of his loneliness. He makes a tentative move toward her, and she reacts as virtually everyone else does—screaming in horror.

The real horror in these films consists not of makeup and special effects but of these terrible moments of rejection. It's no surprise that among the films of the monster film cycle of the fifties were *I Was a Teenage Werewolf* (with Michael Landon) and *I Was a Teenage Frankenstein*. Perhaps the prospect that our love will be unreturned is the scariest thought of all.

*King Kong: DIRECTOR: Merian C. Cooper, Ernest B. Schoedsack WITH: Fay Wray, Bruce Cabot, Robert Armstrong, "Kong, Eighth Wonder of the World"*

*Bride of Frankenstein: DIRECTOR: James Whale WITH: Boris Karloff, Elsa Lanchester, Colin Clive, O. P. Heggie, Una O'Connor*

# Laura (1944)

Homicide detective Mark McPherson (Dana Andrews) has a crush on Laura Hunt (Gene Tierney), the victim in his latest murder case. Without the luxury of fantasy—as in *The Ghost and Mrs. Muir* (1947) or *Portrait of Jennie* (1948)—*Laura* has to come up with a realistic solution to the problem of how to consummate a relationship with someone who is dead.

As Mark interviews the suspects we see, in flashbacks, what a beautiful, vibrant woman Laura was. He learns all he can about her, reading her private diary and personal letters, searching her apartment, and questioning everyone who knew her. He stares longingly at her portrait over the mantelpiece, wishing he could have known her.

"You better watch out, McPherson, or you'll wind up in a psychiatric ward. I don't think they've ever had a patient who fell in love with a corpse," says Waldo Lydecker (Clifton Webb), the waspish radio personality who took Laura under his wing. Waldo was in love with her as well, recalling that "the way she listened was more eloquent than speech."

There's also her weak-willed fiancé, Shelby Carpenter (Vincent Price), who loved her for her kindness, but not enough to keep him from dating one of the models at the ad agency where they worked. Like Mark and Waldo, Shelby's love for Laura seems to be one that centers on how she fulfilled his own needs.

Director Otto Preminger (who took over the film from an ailing Rouben Mamoulian) etches a tale of obsessive love, which is thrown into sharp relief when the object of everyone's affections—Laura—suddenly turns out to be alive. Indeed, she appears to have had the means, motive, and opportunity to commit the murder (of Shelby's mistress, it turns out) herself.

As writer Julie Kirgo notes in *Film Noir: An Encyclopedic Reference to the American Style*, the men in this film are obsessed with "the Laura that each creates in his own mind." For Waldo and Shelby this is at least partially defensible, since they actually knew Laura. Yet Mark's obsession is less explicable. Until her unexpected return from the "dead," he has known her only through the eyes of others.

Mark is a committed detective, doing whatever he has to in order to break the case. His infatuation with Laura might be considered a by-product of his work, but Waldo suspects something more. Jealous of this unexpected rival, Waldo tells Laura, "You were unobtainable when he thought you were dead. That's when he wanted you most."

Ironically, the only obsession the film unambiguously condemns is Waldo's; he has wit and power but lacks the athletic build he demeans in Mark and Shelby. ("I hope you'll never regret what promises to be a disgustingly earthy relationship," he sneers when Laura chooses Mark over him.) The script by Jay Dratler, Samuel Hoffenstein, and Betty Reinhardt (based on the novel by Vera Caspary) even suggests that it is Waldo who is unbalanced. After he faints upon seeing Laura again, he apologizes: "I hope you'll forgive my touch of epilepsy, my dear—an old family custom."

Upon closer inspection, however, *Laura* is a bit too eager to gloss over Mark's unhealthy fixation in order to focus on the romance. Indeed, it's interesting comparing Mark with Scottie Ferguson, the James Stewart character in *Vertigo* (1958), who is also in love with a "dead" woman. *Vertigo*'s Madeleine (Kim Novak) ends up dying not once but twice, and Scottie is driven to the verge of another breakdown; Laura's return from the dead allows Mark to save her in time for a conventional happy ending.

There's something romantic about Mark's devotion to Laura, and to the notion that love can conquer all, even the grave. Yet Waldo is right that there is something a bit unnerving about it as well. Perhaps that's why most films about love "beyond the dark shadow of death" remain in the realm of fantasy: by being reassured it's not real, we can relax and simply enjoy the love affair.

*DIRECTOR: Otto Preminger WITH: Dana Andrews, Gene Tierney, Clifton Webb, Vincent Price*

# Double Indemnity (1944)

When writer/director Billy Wilder was honored by the American Film Institute, one of the speakers was Fred MacMurray. The genial actor noted that twice in his career he was cast against type (both times as an adulterer) and each time it was Wilder who was at the helm. Wilder must have known something that eluded him, suggested MacMurray, for it is his performances in *Double Indemnity* and *The Apartment* that are the best remembered of all his screen roles.

As Walter Neff in *Double Indemnity* (with Wilder and Raymond Chandler adapting James M. Cain's hardboiled novel), MacMurray is a razor-sharp insurance salesman who goes to the Dietrichson household to renew some insurance policies. There he is greeted by a sunbathing Phyllis Dietrichson (Barbara Stanwyck) wearing nothing but a smile and a towel. ("I'd hate to think of your having a smashed fender or something when you're not fully covered," says Walter.) Before long Walter and Phyllis are plotting to murder her husband and collect under the "double indemnity" clause in his life insurance policy.

Their "smart" dialogue shows they're made for each other. In their initial encounter Walter remarks on the "honey of an anklet" she's wearing. When she insists that Walter come back when her husband is home, he asks if she'll be wearing the anklet again. "I wonder if I know what you mean," she says, showing him to the door.

"I wonder if you wonder," he answers with a smile.

Their relationship is a dark parody of domesticity. They have secret meetings at the supermarket, and he calls her "baby." When they decide to murder her husband, their deal is sealed with a kiss.

The conscience of the film is Barton Keyes (Edward G. Robinson), an investigator who treats Walter like a son and who can't let a phony claim get past his desk. Suspecting that Dietrichson's death was murder, he imagines Phyllis and her accomplice thinking they've gotten away with it: "It's not like taking a trolley ride together where they can get off at different stops. They're stuck with each other and they've got to ride all the way 'till the end of the line . . . and the last stop is the cemetery."

Prophetic words indeed, for as with so many murdering movie couples, romance goes out the window once they've committed their foul deed. From the crime that binds, their relationship shifts to looking out for number one. By the time of their final confrontation, whatever feelings of trust that existed between them are long gone.

The revelations are less important than the fact that Walter and Phyllis have changed from lovers to two people ready to kill each other. Phyllis confesses, "No, I never loved you, Walter, not you or anybody else . . . until a minute ago when I couldn't fire that second shot. I never thought that could happen to me."

We can't be sure that Phyllis, unlike Matty from *Body Heat* (1981), isn't finally breaking down and admitting that Walter has gotten through her defenses. It's no dice. With a kiss and a shot, Walter says, "Goodbye, baby."

Some *films noirs* of the forties and fifties give the leads a chance at repentance and renewal. In *The Big Sleep* (based on one of Chandler's Philip Marlowe novels), the double–dealing character played by Lauren Bacall is forgiven because she did it all to protect her wayward sister.

Not here. When love is based on murder, it can only come to a bad end. As Barton tells Walter, "They may think it's twice as safe because they're two of 'em, but it isn't twice as safe—it's ten times twice as dangerous."

*DIRECTOR: Billy Wilder WITH: Barbara Stanwyck, Fred MacMurray, Edward G. Robinson*

# To Have and Have Not (1945)

"You know you don't have to act with me, Steve. You don't have to say anything, and you don't have to do anything. Not a thing. Oh, maybe, just whistle. You know how to whistle, don't you, Steve? You just put your lips together and blow."

On the short list of the most memorable moments in movie history, this scene between Humphrey Bogart and Lauren Bacall has a special place. Not only is there an obvious chemistry between the characters onscreen, but Bogart and Bacall were igniting sparks offscreen as well.

Curiously, there's more going on here than Bacall's suggestive remarks about what he can do with his lips ("It's even better when you help," she says after they kiss). Play and teasing are obviously important for the two characters—which is odd when one remembers the context for the scene: Howard Hawks's drama about the Resistance against the Nazis in wartime Martinique.

Bogart's character is not named Steve, but Harry Morgan, an independent sea captain who charters his boat to tourists for fishing trips. "I can't afford to get mixed up in your local politics," he tells his friends. Enter Marie Browning (Bacall), an independent-minded young woman who has no need to get bogged down with a romance in Vichy-run Martinique when she can go back to the relative safety of the States.

Their seeming rightness for each other is demonstrated in a number of ways, from their arch dialogue to their nicknames for each other. Without explanation, she calls him "Steve" throughout the film, and he calls her "Slim." Marie is also among the few people accepted by Harry's addled friend Eddy (Walter Brennan).

Eddy is an old rummy whom Harry looks after, and whose question "Was you ever bit by a dead bee?" serves as a password into Harry's world. People who dismiss Eddy are unworthy of Harry's support. Marie playfully answers, "Was you?" (Indeed, Marie gets so good at Eddy's nonsense that *Eddy* gets confused: "I feel like I was talking to myself.")

Once the alliance is made, the Nazi-backed Vichy French are helpless against Harry, Marie, Eddy and all that is good and true in the world. We watch *To Have and Have Not* today not because of the story but because it is one of those rare films in which we know that the romance is the real McCoy.

The genesis of the movie is also the stuff of Hollywood legend. In his book-length interview with writer Joseph McBride, director Howard Hawks recounts how he told Ernest Hemingway, "I can make a movie out of the worst thing you ever wrote," which he claimed was "that piece of junk called *To Have and Have Not*." Borrowing little more than the title and a couple of characters, Hawks (and writers Jules Furthman and William Faulkner) created a whole new story.

Hawks also had to create Lauren Bacall out of nineteen-year-old model Betty Bacall (née Betty Persky). After he convinced her she needed a deeper voice, Bacall spent weeks reading aloud in the Hollywood Hills, working on her voice until it reached the proper register. Hawks also told Furthman he wanted to make her character "insolent, as insolent as Bogart, [someone] who insults people, who grins when she does it and people like it."

Not only did people like it, they loved it. Bacall went on to a successful stage and screen career, following up *To Have and Have Not* with *The Big Sleep*, again working for Hawks opposite Bogart. One can see why Hawks was eager to reunite them. Said the director, "When two people are falling in love with each other, they're not tough to get along with, I can tell you that."

*DIRECTOR: Howard Hawks WITH: Humphrey Bogart, Lauren Bacall, Walter Brennan, Hoagy Carmichael, Marcel Dalio, Sheldon Leonard*

# The Lady from Shanghai (1948)

As a love story told in the form of a mystery, *The Lady from Shanghai* is nowhere as exciting as how it got made in the first place.

The intrigue behind the film begins in Boston in 1947. Orson Welles, then separated from Columbia Pictures' reigning love goddess, Rita Hayworth, was involved in a doomed stage production of *Around the World in 80 Days* with producer Mike Todd (who would eventually make the film version in 1956). Hours before curtain, the costume house refused to deliver their wares unless a $50,000 debt was paid. A frantic Welles phoned Harry Cohn, head of Columbia, offering to direct and write a film starring his wife if Cohn would bail him out. When Cohn demanded specifics, Wells glanced at a pulp novel lying on a nearby table: *The Lady from Shanghai*.

Cohn bought the book and Welles used only the title, writing an original screenplay (taking no directing credit) that would become one of his most romantic—and therefore atypical—pictures.

"When I start out to make a fool of myself, there's very little can stop me," says Welles as Michael "Black Irish" O'Hara, relating how a meeting with Elsa Bannister (Hayworth) led to a series of murders and double-crosses. Among the culprits, who O'Hara likens to sharks feeding on each other, are Elsa's sleazy husband, the criminal lawyer Arthur Bannister (Everett Sloane); Bannister's hyena-like partner, George Grisby (Glenn Arders); Broome, a cleanup man who shadows everyone (Ted De Corsia); and other shady types who inhabit this *noir* world.

The mystery of *The Lady from Shanghai* is as hard for the audience to follow as it is for O'Hara, who finds himself attracted to Elsa but repelled by the danger that swirls around her. What is no mystery, however, is the sheer sex appeal that Hayworth exudes from the screen—ironically, under the direction of the man who no longer wanted to be married to her. Perhaps Welles was trying to work out his own torn relationship with Hayworth: she had married a genius, he had married an icon, but they studiously avoided working together until their marriage was nearly over.

Almost as if to make up for lost time, Welles remade Hayworth's glamour for the film, most notably by bleaching her world-famous red hair to platinum blond. He then stretched her image to absurd lengths, photographing her in awkward repose, through diffusion filters, in overly dramatic back light, and wearing ludicrously glossy makeup. If all the men sharing a scene with her are sweaty, drunk or distorted into gargoyles by wide-angle lenses, Hayworth remains a seductive figure. Even in her death throes—shot and bleeding in an abandoned carnival funhouse—the actress is clearly in agony just to satisfy one of Welles's eccentric camera angles. Nevertheless, she remains lovely, even as her demise is protracted to the point of silliness.

Columbia Pictures wasn't at all pleased at Welles's budget, bloated from $1.25 million to nearly $2 million. Not only did their top star play a heavy, she played no love scenes, only teases. Worst of all, the film made no sense whatever and had to be re-edited and partially reshot before it could be released.

*The Lady from Shanghai* is a seedy film. Despite its romantic settings, it looks ugly and confined, just like its characters, who cannot escape the plots they have devised for others. Yet there is an intensity between O'Hara and Elsa that borders on the perverse. They love and hate each other at the same time; the more O'Hara resists Elsa, the stronger their attraction. Something between them is darker than the sum of their parts; despite this desire, they haven't got a chance.

In real life, the same became true for Hayworth and Welles, whose marriage finished with the filming. It could be that Michael O'Hara's last lines about Elsa are those of Welles for Hayworth—a contrived blend of poetry and braggadocio:

"Maybe I'll live so long, I'll forget her. Maybe I'll die tryin'."

*DIRECTOR—WRITER: Orson Welles WITH: Rita Hayworth, Orson Welles, Everett Sloane, Glenn Arders*

# A Place in the Sun (1951)

Are they watching us?" gasps teenage Angela Vickers (Elizabeth Taylor), grabbing a slightly older George Eastman (Montgomery Clift) off the dance floor and leading him into a side room where they can talk in private. As they melt into each other's arms and their beautiful young faces fill the huge screen, these two young lovers create one of Hollywood's most intimate moments. It is also, alas, one of its most tragic, for this pair in *A Place in the Sun* (adapted from Theodore Dreiser's novel, *An American Tragedy*) captures all the promise of a new generation corrupted by the same sins that doomed the old.

The story is relentless: an ambitious son of poor missionaries, George has gotten work at the Eastman swimsuit factory through the kindness of its owner, his estranged Uncle Charles. He immediately breaks their first rule by mixing socially with Alice (Shelley Winters), one of the women who boxes beachwear on the Eastman assembly line. A short time later he gets her "in trouble" (a 1951 code word for "pregnant") and marriage seems to be the only honorable solution, although it would instantly quash his plans for corporate advancement.

Meanwhile, George has met the glamorous Angela, daughter of an industrial magnate. Their infatuation is instant, deep, and dangerous. When Alice threatens to expose George's indiscretion, he plots her murder, then relents (or so he insists at his trial), only to have her drown accidentally.

Irony and romance permeate *A Place in the Sun*. George Stevens—who directs with a poetic if heavy hand—glamorizes the two young people celebrating love (Clift, Taylor) while keeping drab, almost tawdry, the two having sex (Clift, Winters). When Clift visits Taylor they romp with friends and drive in fast cars; this is harshly contrasted with Clift and Winters' secretive, darkened, almost shameful trysts. Irony even surfaces in the songs heard in the background: Clift seduces Winters to "You Made Me Love You" from a small radio; Taylor turns Clift's head to a dance band's "You Came from Out of Nowhere." Faced with such fate, Taylor and Clift's love, despite its photogenic glory, doesn't have a prayer. And since it was born of dishonesty, neither does Clift and Winters'.

There are no traditional villains in this story—no member of the rich Eastman family corrupts George (although their wealth is certainly seductive). George's ambition is neither more nor less than anyone else's. Angela does not purposely tempt him with her carefree lifestyle, but it is clearly part of what George desires—along with possessing her.

*A Place in the Sun* was a bold film in 1951. The decades since have made the screen more frank, but not necessarily more revealing. Winters' gentle, painful performance remains moving, a difficult subject made human. Balanced by the all-consuming love of Clift and Taylor (and who can forget her whispering, as she buries his face in her bosom, "Tell Mama—tell Mama"), *A Place in the Sun* is a reminder that not every great romance ends as it does in the movies. Sometimes they end like in real life.

*DIRECTOR: George Stevens WITH: Elizabeth Taylor, Montgomery Clift, Shelley Winters*

# Vertigo (1958)

*V*ertigo is possibly the most disturbing movie ever made about self-destructive, obsessive, all-consuming love. Rather than focus on the mystery or surprise revelations, director Alfred Hitchcock tosses away the big twist in the story partway through the film, instead focusing on the more interesting twist in the psyche of John "Scottie" Ferguson (James Stewart).

Forced into an aimless retirement from the police after he is discovered to have acrophobia (a fear of heights), he is hired to shadow Madeleine Elster (Kim Novak), a sophisticated, attractive socialite. She is the wife of a friend and has become fixated on a dead ancestor whom she believes to be taking over her body. Scottie follows Madeleine around the city, eventually rescuing her from a suicide leap into San Francisco Bay.

They fall in love, in spite of the fact that her husband is Scottie's friend. Still, she must fulfill her destiny, and she plunges to her death from a church bell tower, which the vertiginous Scottie is unable to climb to save her. Months later, he meets Judy Barton, who bears a striking resemblance to Madeleine. Soon he is changing her hair and makeup and the way she dresses, recreating his lost love through the new person.

At this point the movie plays like *Laura* (1944) in reverse: instead of falling in love with an image and then meeting the real person, Scottie has fallen in love with a real person and is now pursuing the image. Hitchcock (and writers Alec Coppel and Samuel Taylor) now tighten the screws. Judy turns out to *be* Madeleine, at least the Madeleine whom Scottie has known. It was part of a plot to murder the real Madeleine, with Scottie as the gullible witness to her "suicide."

In pursuing the beautiful but unreal Madeleine, Scottie brushes aside the more sensible and down-to-earth Midge (Barbara Bel Geddes), and she disappears partway through the story. Scottie's love can only be called "*l'amour fou*," a mad obsession that ends up destroying both Judy and himself since their only common ground is the shared lie of "Madeleine."

The final third of the film is as powerful as it is emotionally painful. Judy wants to return Scottie's affection, for it was she with whom Scottie fell in love. Yet to reveal that would be to confess to both the betrayal of Scottie and the murder of the real Madeleine. When Scottie finally learns the truth, and exacts his revenge, it is quite possible that he is no longer sane. He insists on a "second chance" as he drags Madeleine/Judy back to the church tower and a dizzying climb that will ultimately lead to one death and—if one cares to speculate what will happen after the closing credits—possibly two.

There is no redemption through love in *Vertigo*, since both the lovers are deeply flawed. This is not a three-hanky picture such as *Magnificent Obsession* (1953), and there is no miraculous last-minute rescue or change of heart. Ultimately, as Hitchcock critic Donald Spoto points out in his *The Art of Alfred Hitchcock*, one is moved by the utter waste of it all.

In another world, under other circumstances, perhaps Scottie and Judy could have found each other and filled the emptiness in each other's life. But here their love, based on lies and deceit, on obsessions and willful blindness, cannot survive.

*DIRECTOR: Alfred Hitchcock WITH: James Stewart, Kim Novak, Barbara Bel Geddes*

# North by Northwest (1959)

Alfred Hitchcock's classic comedy thriller asks you to check your disbelief at the door: twice-divorced ad executive Roger O. Thornhill (Cary Grant) finds himself mistaken for CIA agent George Kaplan and also wanted for the murder—in front of witnesses, yet—of a United Nations diplomat. It's no use going to the police. He's already tried that and even his own mother thinks he's imagining it all.

Roger's salvation will come through meeting the beautiful Eve Kendall (Eva Marie Saint) aboard a Chicago-bound train, and being willing to consider a woman as a partner and helpmate rather than as a fashion accessory. Eve is a classic Hitchcock icy-cool blonde who seems to be attracted to Thornhill *because* he's wanted for murder. "It's going to be a long night, and I don't particularly like the book I started," she says suggestively, inviting him into her sleeper compartment.

Although their passionately lingering kisses went only as far as the Production Code would permit, there is a real conflict here. Roger is desperately in need of an ally to get him out of his predicament, while it is revealed that Eve is working for Roger Vandamm (James Mason), the spy who tried to have Roger killed in the first place. In *North by Northwest* Hitchcock and screenwriter Ernest Lehman rework elements of the director's earlier *Notorious* (1946) to focus on how these characters finally get beyond their secrets to risk trusting someone else. Without such trust, love is impossible.

As Roger's odyssey drags him across the country, he faces more dangers, including being shot at by a crop duster in the middle of a corn field, and a showdown with Vandamm during a public art auction, where he learns that Eve is really a double agent whom he has now compromised. Realizing she is as much a plaything of the spies (theirs *and* ours) as he is, he offers to come to her assistance by pretending to let her kill him at Mount Rushmore. This will presumably get her back in the good graces of the bad guys.

They are then reconciled in a scene in the woods near the monument, the first time they are able to speak to each other honestly. It is a key scene in the picture, since it establishes the bond between them for the remainder of the film, but it almost ended up on the cutting room floor. As Hitchcock retold the story, "My contract had been drawn up by MCA, my agents, and when I read it over, I found that although I hadn't asked for it, they'd put in a clause giving me complete artistic control of the picture. . . . So I was able to say politely, 'I'm very sorry, but this sequence must remain in the picture.'"

If Eve must rescue herself from the passive role that has allowed her to be recruited into becoming a Mata Hari, Roger's adventures constitute a turning away from the thoughtlessness and glibness that has characterized his existence up until now. ("My wives divorced me," he tells Eve during the climactic chase, "I think they said I led too dull a life.")

It is while hanging from atop the Mt. Rushmore monument (actually a studio set) that they must work together and literally reach out for each other. As Thornhill pulls Eve to safety, we dissolve to a cabin on a train, where he is pulling her into a berth they will share. She is now the latest—and presumably the last—Mrs. Thornhill.

The final shot is a train going into a tunnel, of which Hitchcock joked, "There are no symbols in *North by Northwest*. Oh yes! One. The last shot, the train entering the tunnel after the love scene between Grant and Eva Marie Saint. It's a phallic symbol. But don't tell anyone."

*DIRECTOR: Alfred Hitchcock WITH: Cary Grant, Eva Marie Saint, James Mason, Martin Landau, Leo G. Carroll, Jessie Royce Landis, Edward Platt*

# Bonnie and Clyde (1967)

"They're young, they're in love . . . and they kill people."
—advertising slogan for *Bonnie and Clyde*

Few films have so effectively shaken up the art of cinema as *Bonnie and Clyde*, Arthur Penn's unsettling story of two wildcat gangsters who robbed banks and shot people in the Depression-era Southwest. As the title characters, Faye Dunaway and Warren Beatty—fire and ice, respectively—first make crime look like fun, then turn fatalistic once they achieve the fame they had yearned to have for so long but then found frighteningly hollow.

Although it is remembered as a violent drama, *Bonnie and Clyde* is really a love story. From their first meeting when Clyde Barrow shows Bonnie Parker his gun—and soon afterward rejects her sexual advances with "I ain't much of a lover boy . . . I never saw no percentage in it"—it is clear that sex and violence will take on new meaning.

As we later learn in a steamy motel scene, Clyde is as impotent as Bonnie is oversexed. Several robberies and killings later—many serving as release after varying levels of arousal—things have changed. But by then, we know they are doomed.

Perversely, they assemble their family before the "marriage" is consummated. In short order they acquire a brother, Buck (Gene Hackman); a sister (Buck's wife, Blanche, played by Estelle Parsons); and a child, C. W. Moss (Michael J. Pollard).

But it is love—their own brand of it—that drives Bonnie and Clyde, and the film chronicles their odd courtship. At first warming to Clyde when she sees his vulnerability, Bonnie wonders why he prefers to spend so much time with his brother, Buck, and Buck's shrill, petty wife, Blanche. He responds with a cryptic, "Well, I always feel like we're alone," which mollifies her. She later tests his jealousy by kissing a captured Sheriff Frank Hamer (Denver Pyle), whom they tie up and force to pose for snapshots. And together they kidnap and chide (but inwardly admire) two young lovers (Gene Wilder and Evans Evans), only to abandon them once they learn he is an undertaker.

Hard times produce hard people, and *Bonnie and Clyde* is about both. Despite the glossy photography (which won Burnett Guffey an Oscar) and playful bluegrass soundtrack music, the hunger that unites Bonnie and Clyde is that for fame, no matter how fleeting. It is all they have ever had that makes them feel special or alive, and like a shared secret, it unites them as strongly as any other passion. It is as though by living outside the law they also must live outside its sacraments.

At the end, when they realize they have been lured into an ambush and will die within seconds (in one of the movies' most graphic and yet poetic moments), they quickly look at each other. It's only for an instant, but in that exchange can be seen the kind of emotion that people write operas about. It is not fear; it is love.

*DIRECTOR: Arthur Penn WITH: Warren Beatty, Faye Dunaway, Gene Hackman, Estelle Parsons, Michael J. Pollard*

# Body Heat (1981)

When it gets hot, says police detective Oscar Grace (J. A. Preston), "people think the old rules are not in effect." That's what happens to struggling Florida lawyer Ned Racine (William Hurt) in this steamy film that marked the debuts of actress Kathleen Turner and director Lawrence Kasdan.

One night Ned meets the sultry Matty Walker (Turner), who is literally hot—her body temperature runs a degree or two above normal. Matty plays the neglected housewife to her businessman husband Edmund (Richard Crenna), and seduces Ned into a torrid affair that almost burns up the screen. How convenient it would be if hubby would just disappear.

This sounds like a virtual remake of *Double Indemnity* (1944), but *Body Heat* has something else on its mind. In *Double Indemnity*, Fred MacMurray and Barbara Stanwyck are manipulating each other, and the audience is hardpressed to decide who is guiltier. In *Body Heat* there's never any question that Ned is in over his head.

"You're not too smart, are you?" says Matty in brushing off his first overture. "I like that in a man."

Indeed, that's precisely what this *femme fatale* likes. We later learn that Ned and Edmund are just the latest in a long line of men. She fulfills their deepest fantasies by allowing each to think that *he* is the one to finally tame this wild woman ("I never wanted it like this before," she tells Ned after an especially passionate bout of lovemaking).

If ever there was a love of the damned, this is it. Ned accidentally runs into Matty and her husband one night in a restaurant and gets invited to dinner. We are at once appalled at the sort of sleazy high-stakes businessman Edmund is, and equally surprised to see he is nothing like Matty has depicted him. If he had been dealt different cards, Ned could have been another Edmund.

After the murder their conspiracy falls apart. Ned and Matty become the chief suspects, especially when a new will comes to light with an error—an error that leaves Matty as sole beneficiary. If this comes as a surprise to Ned (*he's* listed as the lawyer on the will), he gets even more nervous when a local arsonist (Mickey Rourke) tells him that Matty came around wanting to learn how to set off a timed explosive.

Their final confrontation is heartbreaking. He suspects—in his heart he *knows*—that she's trying to kill him and cover her traces, and yet he is so enraptured by her that he can't stop himself from listening to her.

"I could never do anything to hurt you. I love you," she pleads. "You've got to believe that."

"Keep talking, Matty," he answers. "Experience has shown I can be convinced of *anything*."

Ultimately he pays for their crimes, and finally learns the truth of Matty's past. And we last see Matty with her latest conquest, sitting bored under the hot sun of some unnamed tropical beach.

Hurt, Turner, and director Kasdan say they'll never return to this story, but when they were reunited on the set of *The Accidental Tourist* (1988), the two performers played a little joke on the director. As the filming of one scene began, they shifted into their earlier roles. Matty expressed surprise in seeing him and Ned reminded her that he had promised to follow her to the ends of the Earth.

Perhaps a better answer is offered in the film *Black Widow* (1986), in which a Matty Walker–like character (played by Turner lookalike Theresa Russell) decides the only thing to do after marrying and murdering a man for his money is to continue doing it. As Ned says to Matty near the end of *Body Heat*, "You never quit, do you? You just keep on coming."

*DIRECTOR: Lawrence Kasdan WITH: William Hurt, Kathleen Turner, Richard Crenna, J. A. Preston, Ted Danson*

# CHAPTER EIGHT

# My Funny Valentine

*Romantic comedies are among Hollywood's most enduring love stories, and no wonder. When witty people get together in funny situations and let their hearts (and mouths) run free, there's no telling what kind of screen mischief they can get into.*

# City Lights (1931)

Y ou ain't heard nothin' yet," said Al Jolson in *The Jazz Singer* (1927), and he was right. Within two years, the talkies were king and silent movies—an art that had been developing for more than two decades—were no more.

Perhaps it is the universality of comedy that allowed Charlie Chaplin, alone among the Hollywood stars, to remain silent when audiences demanded that everyone else speak or get off the screen. *The Circus*, released a few months after *The Jazz Singer*, could be excused for its silence, but by 1931 Chaplin wasn't merely bucking a trend, he was a lone (silent) voice. When Chaplin told an interviewer that he would never talk ("For me, it would be fatal"), he was greeted with derision by Jolson. "If Charlie Chaplin doesn't make talkies, he won't make anything."

Undaunted, Chaplin made *City Lights* with music and some sound effects but no dialogue, and produced a film that many consider his finest work. It is a romantic comedy that leaves audiences gasping for breath from laughter one moment and moved to tears the next.

Once again Chaplin plays his beloved Little Tramp, the hapless fellow who is buffeted by fate but remains filled with optimism and good will. One day he buys a flower from a blind girl (Virginia Cherrill) who mistakes him for a man of means. He is able to carry out the charade through the friendship of a millionaire (Harry Myers), a lush who, when sober, can't recall knowing Charlie.

What is touching here is that the Little Tramp is constantly reaching out to help those even less fortunate than himself, whether it is the drunken millionaire trying to jump in a river or the blind girl hoping against hope that she can raise the money for a sight-restoring operation. Perhaps she will even return his love.

After Charlie gets the money from the millionaire, he is mistakenly accused of stealing it. He manages to flee the police long enough to give the money to the flower girl, but then he is arrested and jailed. From slapstick comedy, Chaplin shifts to one of the most ambiguous yet romantic moments in the movies.

Released from jail, Charlie tracks down the flower girl, who can now see and has her own flower shop. He is afraid to do more than stare at her through the window, since he is now shabbier than he was before. She goes out to give him a handout and, in placing the money in his hand, recognizes him by touch.

"You?" she asked him via title card.

"You can see now?"

"Yes, I can see now."

What will happen next? Can they build a relationship based on what they had before? Will she be obliged to him for restoring her sight at great personal sacrifice, or will she reject the possibility of romance with such an abject creature? And should he expect her to ignore his present circumstances or should he sacrifice his feelings by silently stealing away?

Chaplin understood that no matter what alternative he chose, it would ring false. Rather than impose an ending to this impossible romance, he leaves them at the climactic moment: she filled with a mixture of gratitude and confusion, he with devotion and an expression asking if he dare hope for love.

Talk? What could they possibly say? Chaplin had triumphantly showed that he had no need for talkies. Indeed, except for a nonsense song in *Modern Times* (1936), he would not speak on screen until 1940, in *The Great Dictator*.

*DIRECTOR: Charles Chaplin WITH: Charlie Chaplin, Virginia Cherrill, Harry Myers*

# My Man Godfrey (1936)

*My Man Godfrey* is the answer to what happens when an immovable object meets an irresistible force: something's got to give. Godfrey (William Powell) is a surprisingly erudite derelict who lives in a riverside dump near a posh Manhattan neighborhood. Irene Bullock (Carole Lombard) is a scatterbrained heiress who always knows what *she's* doing and can't understand when other people can't keep up.

Irene is out on a charity scavenger hunt and needs a "forgotten man." Having been rudely addressed by Irene's haughty sister Cornelia (Gail Patrick), Godfrey agrees to help Irene. By making this small step, Godfrey is caught in Irene's whirlwind, and it takes him the rest of the film to realize that he's not going to be able to escape. Even when they are married at the final fadeout, he seems dazed.

"Stand still, Godfrey," she says, taking his hand. "It'll all be over in a minute."

Godfrey turns out to be Godfrey Parks ("one of the Boston Parkses"), who left his wealthy and socially connected family following an irresponsible youth and a bad love affair. Unlike his neighbors at the dump, Godfrey has a choice and has chosen to run away from his problems. When Irene offers him a job as butler, he decides that a clean bed and a hot meal don't sound so bad after all.

The Bullock household desperately needs the stability that Godfrey offers. Besides the impulsive Irene and her snobbish sister Cornelia, there is also Mrs. Bullock (Alice Brady), who is even more flighty than Irene, and her artistic "protégé" Carlo (Mischa Auer), who has latched on to a good thing and plays it for all it's worth. As Mr. Bullock (Eugene Pallette) observes, "All you need to start an asylum is an empty room and the right kind of people."

By film's end Godfrey has saved Mr. Bullock's investments, taught Cornelia humility, and regained his self-respect. Even Mrs. Bullock will have to learn to make do without Carlo. The only one who is largely unchanged is Irene. While she has learned some sense of responsibility for others, that idea was largely in place from the beginning; early on she explains the importance of Godfrey becoming *her* protégé by telling him, "Not only does it occupy my mind, but it's character–building, too."

Throughout, she remains in her own scatterbrained world. When Godfrey sees through the latest of her attention-getting acts by unceremoniously dumping her into a cold shower, it is all she can do to contain herself. "Godfrey loves me," she shouts, utterly convinced that his rejection is indeed proof of his love.

But that's precisely what it is in this madcap world, and those critics who argue that Godfrey and Irene are going to turn into another version of the Bullocks are merely being churlish. Godfrey needs Irene's unpredictability just as she needs his steadying hand. Together they'll fight the Depression at The Dump, the chic restaurant staffed by other "forgotten men" that he's built on the landfill where they first met.

Their renewed commitment to the world around them makes this more than just a story about immature lovers. In 1957 the film was remade with David Niven and June Allyson, but absent the social context, the result was no more than entertaining fluff.

The chemistry between Powell and Lombard here is especially interesting when one remembers that they had been married and divorced a few years before. They had remained friends, and when he was loaned to Universal Pictures by MGM for *My Man Godfrey*, Powell, ever the gentleman, insisted that the part of Irene go to his ex-wife.

*DIRECTOR: Gregory La Cava WITH: William Powell, Carole Lombard, Gail Patrick, Eugene Pallette, Alice Brady, Mischa Auer*

# The Shop Around the Corner (1940)

Aman and woman fall in love as pen pals, not realizing that they are the same coworkers who can't stand each other face to face. From this simple situation, writer Samson Raphaelson (adapting Nikolaus Laszlo's play) and director Ernst Lubitsch skillfully serve up one of the movies' most charming love stories.

James Stewart is the officious but fair shop manager of a small Budapest department store owned by Frank Morgan. He hires, and is initially drawn to, the opinionated Margaret Sullavan. Their mutual attraction quickly dissipates when they clash over sales techniques.

At the same time, their pseudonymical postal correspondence has drawn them together. Eventually an assignation is arranged, then canceled.

It is only when Stewart discovers the truth that he is attracted to Sullavan in person and must figure out how to salvage the romance. He does, thanks to "the Lubitsch touch."

Much has been written about the celebrated Lubitsch touch, but in today's more crass world it is difficult to explain. What German expatriate director Lubitsch did was to place his characters in highly charged situations and have them act as though they knew the audience was already on their side. This technique created a warmth and affinity as well as, at times, screen poetry. In *The Shop Around the Corner*, for example, the poetry surfaces in behavior: Margaret Sullavan visits her mailbox only to find it empty. We see only her hand—first expectant, then groping, then dropping, limp and dejected. We can imagine her lovely face glowing in anticipation of a new missive, then wondering where it is, and finally frowning over being forgotten.

The method triumphs again in the glee we and the store employees feel when Stewart fires a clerk (Joseph Schildkraut) who has been having an affair with the boss's wife. The clerk never admits to it, but everybody already knows, and his dismissal is icing on their cake. And there is a running gag in which meek Felix Bressart finds new ways to bolt from the room whenever Frank Morgan wants to know what his employees think about new merchandise. Naturally, the only ones who offer an opinion are Stewart and Sullavan, which only increases their conflict. But by now the audience is ahead of them: we want them to reconcile, but how?

The filmmakers' skills are is most evident in the complex final scene that brings them together. Consider the elements: Stewart has to (a) talk Sullavan out of being in love with the pen pal she has still not met; (b) convince her that he is worth loving instead; (c) confess to her that he, in truth, is her pen pal; while (d) distracting her from realizing that he has, in effect, purposely misled her; and (e) prevent the audience from hating him *and* thinking Sullavan is stupid for accepting it.

The plot of *The Shop Around the Corner* proved so durable that it was remade as a Judy Garland–Van Johnson musical in 1949, *In the Good Old Summertime*. With the gimmick of a telephone party line substituting for love letters, it even lent its spirit to *Pillow Talk* in 1959. Presumably, the next update will bring it into the fax generation.

*DIRECTOR: Ernst Lubitsch WITH: James Stewart, Margaret Sullavan, Frank Morgan, Joseph Schildkraut, Felix Bressart*

# The Lady Eve (1941)

For the first four years of the 1940s, writer-director Preston Sturges owned Hollywood. His string of finely tuned, wise and crackly romantic comedies (*The Great McGinty*, *Christmas in July*, *Sullivan's Travels*, *The Palm Beach Story*, *Miracle of Morgan's Creek*, *Hail the Conquering Hero*) is unrivaled. Unfortunately, Sturges knew it, and acted as though Newton's law of gravity somehow didn't apply to his career.

By the end of World War II Sturges's light had dimmed, though not burned out entirely; in the way Hollywood has of watching those it envies twist in the wind, it reduced him to flickering at its periphery for another ten years. Not until the 1970s was his work noticed and exalted by a new generation dulled by television sitcoms—an irony that Sturges would have savored had he been alive.

*The Lady Eve* was one of the prime rediscoveries. Sandwiched between the better-known *Sullivan's Travels* (1941) and *The Palm Beach Story* (1942), this fast-paced romp about a female swindler (Barbara Stanwyck), her card-shark father (Charles Coburn), and a shy snake expert (Henry Fonda) became a hit all over again, and no wonder.

Typically, Sturges backs into this trap-strewn arena. His father-daughter-butler (Melville Cooper) team operates aboard cruise ships, where their sole purpose is to separate the well-heeled set from their mad money. When Fonda boards mid-ocean following a zoological expedition, Stanwyck gloms on to his "fine specimen of the sucker sapiens" like snake to apple. Soon, to her own surprise (and her father's consternation), she really and truly falls for him.

"You're certainly a funny girl for anybody to meet who's just been up the Amazon for a year," whimpers Fonda to Stanwyck, without the faintest clue that she and her father are about to soak him for his family's brewery fortune.

"Good thing you weren't up there for two years," she says, starting a seduction that will unexpectedly draw her in for real. For *The Lady Eve* is not a cynical crime caper, it's a love story.

But there's always a serpent in the garden—in this case Stanwyck's past, which is leaked to the trusting Fonda by his rough-edged valet, Ambrose Murgatroyd (William Demarest). Once the snake is out of the bag, Fonda shuns Stanwyck, and it takes the rest of the film to throw them back together—and even then there's a final joke at fadeout that has raised eyebrows for half a century.

Stanwyck and Fonda's sustained brilliance allowed Sturges to indulge in long, devilishly constructed takes that were simultaneously sexy and funny. Their first shipboard tryst winds up in her cabin (his pet snake having scared her out of his), where she caresses his cheek, twists his hair (and him) around her little finger, and then reports innocently, "You better go to bed, Hopsy, I think I can sleep peacefully now," knowing full well that, thanks to her, he cannot.

Unlike most of Preston Sturges's other films, *The Lady Eve* supposedly had no message, but it does. It says that in the battle of the sexes, straight truth is better ammunition, even if deception is sometimes more fun.

*DIRECTOR-WRITER: Preston Sturges WITH: Barbara Stanwyck, Henry Fonda, Charles Coburn*

# Pillow Talk (1959)

In the late 1960s it became fashionable, even expected, to make fun of Doris Day and the frothy sex comedies she dominated since 1959's *Pillow Talk*. To a youth-oriented culture bent on breaking from the Establishment by growing long hair, smoking dope and practicing free love, the conservative morality represented by Day and her frequent co-star Rock Hudson seemed ludicrously outdated. But producer Ross Hunter knew better.

"No one guessed that under all those dirndls lurked one of the wildest asses in Hollywood," he later insisted, and from the way he crafted this and other Doris Day pictures it was clear Hunter knew what was going on in the audience's minds.

And in the audience's minds is exactly where *Pillow Talk* plays.

Like *The Shop Around the Corner*, it is about alter egos: Day and Hudson are feuding customers who share a telephone party line. When Hudson finally sees Day in person (thanks to Tony Randall, who happens to be their mutual friend), he poses as a Texas businessman and woos her. Hudson dares not reveal his deceit when they actually fall in love. To make matters worse, Randall is smitten with Day and does everything he can to expose Hudson's ruse. The only other element the film needs is a wisecracking housekeeper—and that's why God created Thelma Ritter.

Nothing in *Pillow Talk* gets in the way of reality. Everybody in it has enough money to dress well, decorate well (clothes and sets are hallmarks of Ross Hunter pictures), party well and take cabs everywhere. Of course, everyone has a white telephone, and the visual party-line gags—all of which are lost when this CinemaScope film is seen on television—involve split screens in which Day and Hudson appear to share bed and bath but of course don't.

What remains attractive about *Pillow Talk* is its sheer innocence despite an underlying rumble of sexuality. All the characters clearly *know* about sex, but they are mature enough to postpone it. Compare that with today's smarmy youth comedies in which sex is the joke itself and soon becomes boring.

Hudson and Day's light touch is what keeps their work (which also includes *Lover Come Back*, 1962, and *Send Me No Flowers*, 1964), appealingly clean. The dark thoughts are left to Randall as Day's would-be suitor and Ritter as her perennially hungover maid. Through the use of voice-overs and sassy asides as well as crisp dialogue, one is reminded that movie love used to be fun.

But then, much of *Pillow Talk* is literally a time capsule. Nobody has party lines any more. Nobody who lives that well could work so little. And most dated of all are New Yorkers who could be that naïve. Hudson wins Day with deception; what kind of way is this to begin a true relationship? Then again, like James Stewart in *The Shop Around the Corner*, he finally comes clean, and it is this display of honesty that seals the friendship.

Despite (or perhaps because of) its veneer of purity, *Pillow Talk* is as refreshing today as it was when it was on Hollywood's sexual cutting edge. The fact that it was carried out with a gentle wink to the audience, and not a leer, makes it impossible to mock; quite to the contrary, it once again has a lot to admire. Thirty years after it was made—after AIDS (which killed Rock Hudson) and other sexually transmitted diseases have forced people back into a more conservative "morality"—*Pillow Talk* has, like an old necktie, suddenly come back into style.

*DIRECTOR: Michael Gordon WITH: Rock Hudson, Doris Day, Tony Randall, Thelma Ritter*

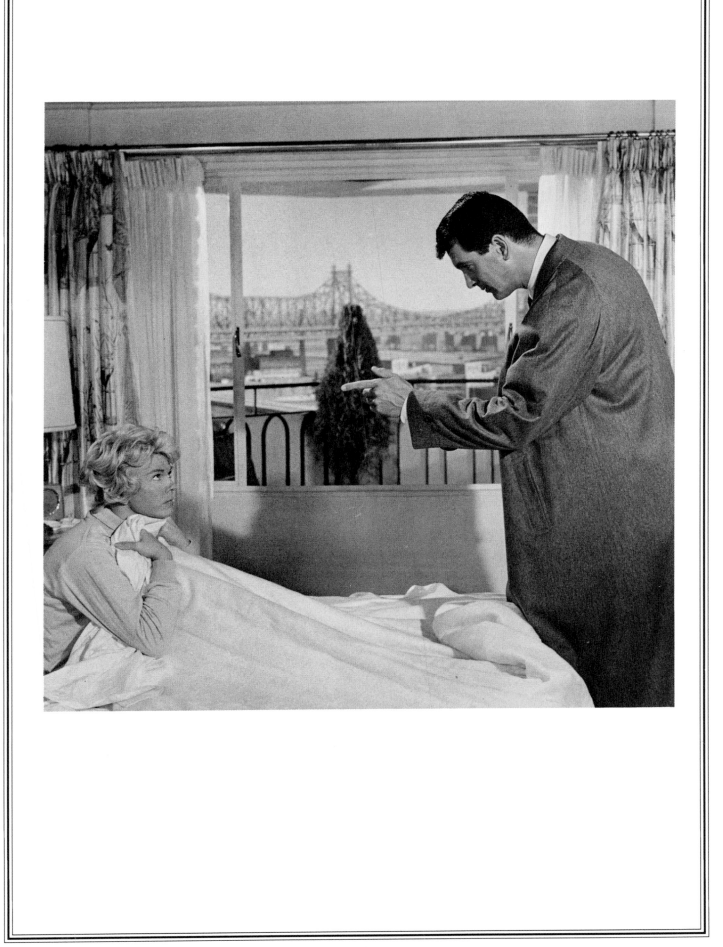

# The Goodbye Girl (1977)

One of the most entertaining romantic comedies of 1977 almost didn't get made at all. Neil Simon's *The Goodbye Girl* originally rolled in 1975 under the title *Bogart Slept Here*, starring Robert De Niro and directed by Mike Nichols. After one week, however, production was called off in the belief that it just wasn't funny to watch a story about an actor who makes it big and then has to deal with success.

Two years later another director, Herbert Ross—who had just successfully filmed Simon's *The Sunshine Boys*—restarted the picture. By then Simon had changed his script to focus on a *struggling* actor (played by Richard Dreyfuss) and this time it was funny enough to keep shooting (and keen-eyed viewers can still spot De Niro on a wall poster that gets hit with a cologne bottle as an inside joke early in the picture).

*The Goodbye Girl* is the stock pairing of two mismatched antagonists lifted to dizzying heights by Simon's perceptive character writing. Dreyfuss is Elliot Garfield, fresh from Chicago to appear in what becomes a bizarre stage production of *Richard III*. When he learns that the apartment he sublet from fellow actor Tony DeForest is still occupied by DeForest's just-jilted girlfriend, Paula McFadden (Marsha Mason), and her twelve-year-old daughter Lucy (Quinn Cummings), it's a demonstration of Newton's first law of rent control: share it or leave it. Naturally, Dreyfuss and Mason instantly clash; only his fondness for Lucy, and hers for him, placate Mason until—by Act Two—love is blooming.

Unlike movies-about-movies that routinely do commercial swan dives, this film-about-theater succeeds. That's because Neil Simon not only understands the milieu, he also knows how to invent people who legitimately embody the glibness and charisma that propel the story.

At first it's all friction, as Paula tries to tell Elliot her rules for sharing the apartment. Quite her match, Elliot counters with *his* rules—among them, he informs her as he inspects the bathroom, "I-don't-like-the-panties-drying-on-the-rod."

But by the time he soothes Lucy's upset stomach half an hour later ("How do you feel?" he asks the girl. She answers, "Did you see *The Exorcist*? Then you better leave the room"), mother and co–tenant start melting some ice. A little later they're having pizza on the roof and dancing to Gershwin.

*The Goodbye Girl* touches all the New York bases: Elliot takes Lucy for a ride around Central Park in a hansom carriage; Paula is mugged outside a liquor store; Elliot's *Richard III* is trashed by the critics; and finally, Paula again must face the possibility that another actor may walk out on her.

Dreyfuss won an Oscar for his work in the film, one of the few movies to have given the brash, intelligent actor an equally brash, intelligent role. Similarly, Mason expertly travels from self-doubt to self-reliance, only occasionally veering into the "I'm happy with myself" attitude that later became her trademark. *The Goodbye Girl* is a snazzy love letter to New York, to theater, to wit, and above all, to second chances.

*DIRECTOR: Herbert Ross WITH: Richard Dreyfuss, Marsha Mason, Quinn Cummings*

# Manhattan (1979)

Once upon a time there was a kingdom called New York City. Those who lived outside its imposing stone walls believed evil to lurk inside, but those who dwelled high atop its towers knew it to be an enchanted realm. Sure, there are crazies, but those who deeply loved New York saw it through the eyes of a lover and overlooked its flaws.

One of those lovers happens to be Woody Allen. In his films, he "idealized it out of all proportion," to use the words with which he begins *Manhattan*. Allen's Big Apple has none of the worms and rot that inspire the violent action stories other filmmakers find on its mean streets; for Allen, New York is "the city of his dreams" to which he is constantly sending cinematic love letters.

This adoration is articulated through its people—a glib, upscale, usually rich and frequently neurotic set who ignore the petty problems of the city while diligently creating their own.

In *Manhattan*, Allen plays a TV writer who finally becomes disgusted with the banality of his work while enjoying the mentor-lover affair he is having with teenage Mariel Hemingway. When his best friend, Michael Murphy, confesses he has been cheating on his wife with a high-strung freelance writer, Diane Keaton, Allen is instantly judgmental. Yet no sooner do Murphy and Keaton break up than Allen is, to his own surprise, dating her. Making a stab at morality, he dumps Hemingway—right before Keaton starts seeing Murphy again.

It sounds like an urban daisy chain, but *Manhattan*'s characters aren't really looking for love or sex, Allen argues, as much as distracting themselves from issues that loom more frightening, such as Death. At once he and co-screenwriter Marshall Brickman are perceptively charting a sequence of human relationships among modern, civilized people and also arguing that *all* human relationships are merely what we do to keep busy until we die. The only things that make life worth living, he lists in a touching monologue, are little ones from which we glean private pleasure: the crabs at Sam Wo's, Louis Armstrong's recording of "Potatohead Blues," Groucho Marx, etc.

And Manhattan. The city is more than Allen's movie location; it is a world unto itself of trendy restaurants where the elite graze, of parties, of private schools, of taxis, bookstores, museums, galleries and planetariums, of relaxing with the Sunday *New York Times*.

In Woody Allen's Manhattan people can still walk their dogs at three in the morning and stay out safely to watch the sunrise over the Fifty-ninth Street Bridge. They can quit their job and instantly get a publishing deal; easily change apartments; dine casually at the Russian Tea Room; ride through Central Park in a hansom carriage while Gershwin music defines the pulse of a romantic city—all the trappings of romance and happiness that, by the way, will one day be whisked away by the Grim Reaper.

In a previous film, *Annie Hall*, Allen explained our pursuit of love despite the pain that came with it by joking, "We need the eggs." In *Manhattan* he is saying that even though we might find love. We cannot live by omelets alone.

*DIRECTOR-COWRITER: Woody Allen WITH: Woody Allen, Diane Keaton, Mariel Hemingway, Michael Murphy*

# Arthur (1981)

Arthur's a useless drunk, yet rich and charming; Linda's an actress-waitress who shoplifts a tie for her father. Naturally, they fall in love.

*Arthur* came out of nowhere in 1981 to establish then-new Orion Pictures, baffled all who had ignored the film during production, and enchanted $42 million worth of audiences. They were captivated by Dudley Moore's self-effacing jokes as Arthur Bach, moved by Liza Minnelli's secure but open-minded Linda Marolla, touched by John Gielgud (who won an Oscar for this atypical role) as Arthur's sarcastic valet, Hobson, and dazzled by writer-director Steve Gordon's light romantic touch.

*Arthur* took the old Hollywood convention of mocking the idle rich and gave it a disarming twist by having the rich, through the elfin Moore, make fun of themselves. As a result, audiences readily understood why Arthur drank—he wanted to escape all those stuck-up bluebloods. And even his $750 million inheritance didn't dull the pain of being condemned to marry a numbingly bland debutante (Jill Eikenberry).

It certainly explains Arthur's (and our) affection for Linda. She doesn't want Arthur for his money, although her unemployed father (Barney Martin) has no objection to it. She only wants Arthur to grow up—something that everybody else in the story (Hobson, Aunt Martha, his father) fears he will never do.

Arthur blithely ignores all of them and has so little respect for himself that he can't see the wisdom of their advice. There is, however, a glimmer of hope: Linda. He respects her so much that he rejects the idea of keeping her as his mistress after he marries the deb. This hint of true love is the first clue that Arthur is capable of maturing; later, as he assumes care of the dying Hobson, his movement toward adulthood is assured.

So much about *Arthur* makes it endure as one of the key romantic comedies of the eighties. Dudley Moore's happy drunk and his seemingly endless variations on gags (notably a monologue opposite a stuffed moose) give the film the giddy spontaneity of out-takes. Minnelli, whose waiflike presence too often condemns her to tear-stained roles, here offers a tough counterpart to Moore's scene stealing. And Sir John Gielgud's dignified reading of purposely undignified lines ("Poor drunks do not find love, Arthur. Poor drunks have very few teeth. They urinate outdoors. They freeze to death in the summer. I can't bear to think of you that way.") is yet another poke at wealth, this time from an observer rather than a participant.

As with Woody Allen in *Manhattan*, Steve Gordon in *Arthur* sees New York as paradise. And the Burt Bacharach–Carol Bayer Sager–Christopher Cross Oscar-winning "Arthur's Song" (about being "caught between the moon and New York City") is the icing on a delicious cake.

Alas, nine years later the magic had evaporated. A sequel, *Arthur 2 on the Rocks*, directed by Bud Yorkin, reunited the cast but missed the mark. Part of the explanation lay with society: between 1981 and 1990 alcoholism stopped being funny.

But the true tragedy of *Arthur* is the death of writer-director Steve Gordon in 1981 from a heart attack just as his film was achieving success. He seems to have been the only filmmaker since Blake Edwards (in *10*) to utilize Moore's uniquely winning but easily tiring persona.

The joys in *Arthur* come from puncturing balloons, not poking uninflated ones. Arthur never insults Linda, Hobson, the chauffeur Bitterman (Ted Ross) or anybody else he truly respects. He is not an ingrate, just a child.

As the poor little rich boy, Arthur wins hearts by being helpless, but as he learns in the story, he *keeps* hearts by facing his responsibilities—and by holding onto his $750 million. "After all," he says, "I'm not stupid."

*DIRECTOR: Steve Gordon WITH: Liza Minelli, Dudley Moore, John Gielgud*

# When Harry Met Sally ... (1989)

The success of *When Harry Met Sally . . .* upon its release showed that people still wanted love stories, especially comic ones in which two people end up together because they were meant for each other.

Critics immediately noticed the similarities between *When Harry Met Sally . . .* and the films of Woody Allen. Director Rob Reiner and screenwriter Nora Ephron had obviously been influenced by *Annie Hall* (1977) and *Manhattan* (1979) in telling their tale of two people finding love in a New York filled with great music by Gershwin, Kern, and Rodgers and Hart.

What the critics missed is that the differences are far more interesting than the similarities. Allen's films were essentially downbeat: *Annie Hall* is about the breakup of a relationship, while the most optimistic *Manhattan* gets is a seventeen-year-old girl advising a middle-aged man that "you have to have a little faith in people." What *When Harry Met Sally . . .* is about is a celebration of finding the person with whom you want to share the rest of your life.

Even before we're introduced to the main characters, we meet the first in a series of elderly couples who comically reminisce about how they met. We then see newly minted college graduates Harry (Billy Crystal) and Sally (Meg Ryan) as they're about to travel from Chicago to New York. Harry tells her, "Men and women can't be friends because the sex part always gets in the way." And so they part.

Five years later they meet again, this time on a plane from New York to Washington. Again they mix about as well as oil and water. But those older couples keep appearing and the message is clear. Harry and Sally belong together. They just don't know it yet.

The main thrust of the film is how they become friends, seeing that friendship and love are not mutually exclusive. To relieve themselves of the pressures of a dating relationship, they decide to deny any possibility of romance ("I got married so I could stop dating," admits Harry about his failed marriage).

In the film's most talked-about scene, Sally reveals that women sometimes fake their reactions in bed and that men can't tell the difference. She loudly simulates an orgasm in the middle of a crowded deli, while Harry can just stare in amazement. The capper to the scene is when a customer at the next table (played by Estelle Reiner, the director's mother) tells her server, "I'll have what she's having."

After they finally spend the night together, they both get cold feet. Suddenly they're awkward with each other, neither being quite sure of the other's intentions. When Sally hesitantly suggests it was a mistake, Harry rushes to agree with her so quickly that she is taken aback.

*When Harry Met Sally . . .* concludes with a final interview with a happily married couple—Harry and Sally themselves. And he's agreeing with her about her insistence that food be served just so, in this case the coconut wedding cake with the chocolate sauce "on the side."

Earlier he made fun of her, saying that "*on the side* is a very big thing for you." Now, he's adopting it for himself. That is the sort of optimism that makes this film closer kin to Reiner's earlier *The Sure Thing* (1985) than either of the Allen films. As Harry tells her, "When you realize you want to spend the rest of your life with somebody, you want the rest of your life to start as soon as possible."

*DIRECTOR: Rob Reiner WITH: Billy Crystal, Meg Ryan, Bruno Kirby, Carrie Fisher*

# Bibliography

Allen, Woody. *Four Films of Woody Allen*. New York: Random House, 1982.

Anobile, Richard J., ed. *Michael Curtiz's Casablanca*. New York: Universe Books, 1974.

Anobile, Richard J., ed. *Ernst Lubitsch's Ninotchka*. New York: Flare Books, 1975.

Anobile, Richard J., ed. *Woody Allen's Play It Again, Sam*. New York: Grosset & Dunlap, 1977.

Bayer, William. *The Great Movies*. New York: Grosset & Dunlap, 1973.

Behlmer, Rudy. *Memo from: David O. Selznick*. New York: Grove Press, 1981.

Berg, A. Scott. *Goldwyn: A Biography*. New York: Alfred A. Knopf, 1989.

Curtis, James. *Between Flops: A Biography of Preston Sturges*. New York: Harcourt Brace Jovanovich, 1982.

Davidson, Bill. *Spencer Tracy: Tragic Idol*. New York: E. P. Dutton, 1988.

Dooley, Roger. *From Scarface to Scarlett*. New York: Harcourt Brace Jovanovich, 1984.

Green, Stanley. *Encyclopedia of the Musical Film*. New York: Oxford University Press, 1981.

Halliwell, Leslie. *Halliwell's Filmgoer's Companion*. 9th ed. New York: Charles Scribner's Sons, 1988.

Hardy, Phil. *The Encyclopedia of Science Fiction Movies*. Minneapolis: Woodbury Press, 1986.

Harvey, James. *Romantic Comedy*. New York: Alfred A. Knopf, 1987.

Haver, Ronald. *A Star Is Born: The Making of the 1954 Movie and Its 1983 Restoration*. New York: Alfred A. Knopf, 1988.

Haver, Ronald. *David O. Selznick's Hollywood*. New York: Alfred A. Knopf, 1980.

Kendall, Elizabeth. *The Runaway Bride*. New York: Alfred A. Knopf, 1990.

Maltin, Leonard. *TV Movies and Video Guide*. 1991 edition. New York: Plume, 1990.

Mast, Gerald. *Howard Hawks, Storyteller*. New York: Oxford University Press, 1982.

McBride, Joseph. *Hawks on Hawks*. Berkeley: University of California Press, 1982.

McDonald, Gerald D., Michael Carey and Mark Ricci, eds. *The Films of Charlie Chaplin*. New York: Citadel Press, 1965.

Meyer, Nicholas. *The Love Story Story*. New York: Avon Books, 1971.

Mueller, John. *Astaire Dancing*. New York: Alfred A. Knopf, 1985.

Peary, Danny. *Cult Movies 2*. New York: Dell Publishing Co., 1983.

Peary, Danny. *Cult Movies 3*. New York: Simon & Schuster, 1988.

Rosenblum, Ralph, and Robert Karen. *When the Shooting Stops . . . the Cutting Begins*. New York: Viking Press, 1979.

Schickel, Richard. "The Publisher's Afterword: The Legend as Actress." In *Garbo* by Antoni Gronowicz. New York: Simon & Schuster, 1990.

Sennett, Ted. *Lunatics and Lovers*. New Rochelle, NY: Arlington House, 1973.

Silver, Alain, and Elizabeth Ward. *Film Noir*. Woodstock, NY: The Overlook Press, 1979.

Spoto, Donald. *The Art of Alfred Hitchcock*. New York: Hopkinson and Blake, 1976.

Sturges, Sandy, ed. *Preston Sturges by Preston Sturges: His Life in His Words*. New York: Simon & Schuster, 1990.

Truffaut, Francois. *Hitchcock*. New York: Simon & Schuster, 1967.

Walker, Alexander. *The Shattered Silents*. New York: William Morrow, 1979.

Willis, Donald, ed. *Variety's Complete Science Fiction Reviews*. New York: Garland Publishing, 1985.